SCOUTMASTER MINUTE

YOUR HANDBOOK FOR INSPIRING MOMENTS

RON WENDEL

Gibbs Smith, Publisher
Salt Lake City

Dedicated to the leaders and teachers of the youth.

First Edition
10 09 08 07   7 6 5 4

Text © 2005 by Ron Wendel

Published by
Gibbs Smith, Publisher
P.O. Box 667
Layton, Utah 84041

Orders: (1-800) 748-5439
www.gibbs-smith.com

Designed by Kurt Wahlner
Printed and bound in the United States of America

This is not an official Boy Scouts of America publication.

Library of Congress Cataloging-in-Publication Data
Wendel, Ron.
  Scoutmaster minute / Ron Wendel.--1st ed.
  p. cm.
ISBN 1-58685-461-5
1. Boy Scouts—Conduct of life—Miscellanea. 2. Conduct of life—Quotations, maxims, etc. 3. Scout leaders—Miscellanea. 4. Moral education. I. Title.
HS3312.W46 2005
646.7'00835'1—dc22
                              2004022519

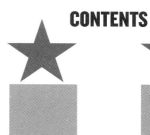

CONTENTS

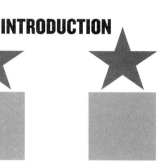

INTRODUCTION

As Scoutmasters and leaders of youth, we have the opportunity to share many exciting experiences with our Scouts. From a hike in the woods to a swim at the local pool, we can enjoy the challenge of teaching them things like nature skills, first aid, lifesaving and personal development. But just as important, we have a responsibility to teach Scouts character, to help them develop standards and build values in their lives.

The Scouting values are summed up in the Scout Oath and Scout Law. Every boy should be "on [his] honor to do [his] best to do [his] duty to God and [his] country, and to obey the Scout Law..." We need to teach Scouts to build their character, strengthen their values and standards, display courage and stand for the right, believe in God, love their country, be kind and fair, and serve others.

The best way to teach any kind of a lesson is with a

story. It doesn't matter how young or old we are, we like to listen to the experiences of others. I'm often surprised at the many times I start to tell a story to a group of restless boys, only to see them quiet down and give me their complete attention.

Good stories aren't hard to find—they are all around us. They regularly appear in the news and in sports, but we can also find them in history and in the lives of famous men and women. Also, many valuable stories can be drawn from our own personal experiences and the world around the boys. Even though a story may be the best way to teach a lesson, sometimes the opportunity presents itself for a thought-provoking question, a quote, or a poem.

Boys love to be taught about the world around them, and they know it is important. They care about what's going on in the world. Scouts also like to know that others care about them, and who they are becoming. By taking a minute or two at the end of a meeting or around a campfire to share your values and ideals, you show the young men that you, as their Scoutmaster, care about them.

—*Ron Wendel*

CHARACTER

A SCOUT IS **TRUSTWORTHY**. A SCOUT TELLS THE TRUTH. HE KEEPS HIS PROMISES. HONESTY IS PART OF HIS CODE OF CONDUCT. PEOPLE CAN DEPEND ON HIM.

A SCOUT IS **LOYAL**. A SCOUT IS TRUE TO HIS FAMILY, FRIENDS, SCOUT LEADERS, SCHOOL, NATION, AND THE COMMUNITY OF THE WORLD.

A SCOUT is at an age where he is growing, developing, learning new skills, and acquiring new talents. Many young men find themselves beginning to excel in sports and academics. As you excel, it is important to remember your standards and values. Achieving success means little without honor. Ability will allow a man to get to the top, but character is the only thing that will keep him there.

—m—

A SCOUT IS TRUSTWORTHY, and a big part of trustworthiness is honesty. Sometimes it is hard to be honest, such as when you must take a test you haven't studied for. At times like that it is even more important to be honest. A science professor at a local university gave a test at the end of each chapter; and included a short thought at the bottom of the test page. On one particular test the message read: "You are taking two tests today: one in physics, and one in honesty. There are many good men and women in the world that cannot pass a test in physics. So if you must fail one of these tests, it is better to fail the physics test."

—m—

A SCOUT IS LOYAL—loyal to God, family, and friends. We show our loyalty by trusting others, believing in them, and always hoping that they believe and trust us. An excellent example of loyalty is seen in the story of Damon and Pythias.

Damon and Pythias were the best of friends. They had grown up together and loved and trusted each other like brothers. However, as they grew older, Pythias began to speak against the King Dionysius, the ruler of their city. He said that an unjust ruler should not have power over others, and that their king was nothing more than a tyrant. As Pythias continued his speeches, the king lost his patience and ordered Pythias arrested and thrown in jail. King Dionysius brought Pythias before him, and asked him to take back his words, but Pythias would not. The king declared Pythias a traitor and sentenced him to die.

The king then asked if Pythias had any last request, whereupon Pythias said that he only wished to go home long enough to say goodbye to his wife and children and to put his things in order. King Dionysius laughed and said, "Not only do you think of me as a tyrant, but you must also take me for a fool. If I let you leave the city, you would escape and never return."

At this point, Damon, who had watched the proceedings, stepped forward and said, "I will be his pledge. I will stay here in Syracuse until Pythias returns. You know of our friendship, and Pythias will return as long as you hold me." The king considered the proposal, and said, "By taking his place, it not only means that you will sit in prison until he returns, but it also means that if he doesn't return by the appointed day, you will also die for him."

Damon replied, "I trust my friend. He will return."

Pythias was allowed to travel to his home, and Damon was thrown in prison. As the days went by, the king saw that Pythias was not coming back, so the king went down to the prison to talk to Damon. King Dionysius said, "The time is almost up, and your friend has not returned. You have been a fool to trust him, and I will not give you any mercy."

To this, Damon bravely replied, "He has been delayed by some accident or misfortune. But I know that if it is within his power, he will be here in time." The king was amazed at the trust Damon had in his friend.

Finally the fateful day arrived. Damon was taken from the prison and brought before the executioner. The king laughed at Damon and said, "What do you think of your friend now? The time has passed, and he has not returned."

No sooner had the king spoken these words, than a shout was heard among the crowd, and Pythias ran up to Damon and embraced him. Pythias explained that his ship had been wrecked in a storm, and bandits had attacked him on the road, yet his only thought was to return in time to save his friend. Pythias turned to the king and said, "I am ready to face my death."

King Dionysius listened to the story with surprise, and then said, "I revoke the sentence. I did not believe that such friendship and loyalty could exist between two friends, and it is only right that you should both be rewarded with your freedom. I only asked one thing—that I too can be part of so worthy of a friendship."

IF YOU'VE EVER LOST a ten-dollar bill, you feel pretty bad. If you lose more money, you feel even worse, but that's nothing compared to how you feel when you're sick or injured. It's especially bad if you find out that your sickness or injury is going to take a long time before you're healed. But there's one thing even worse than losing money or getting sick, and that is losing your integrity. It has been said that when wealth is lost, nothing is lost. When health is lost, something is lost. When character is lost, all is lost.

A SCOUT IS TRUSTWORTHY, and we earn trust through our honest dealings with others. By being honest, we show respect for others; and then because of our honesty, others respect us. Jacob Hamblin (1819-1886, missionary and frontiersman) had a reputation as an honest man among the Indian tribes in his area. Because of his honesty, they respected him.

Jacob Hamblin lived in southern Utah during the late 1800s. This was a time when many of the pioneers and settlers often had trouble with the Indians. Jacob Hamblin was a spokesman for the white men, and because of his honesty he gained the complete confidence of the Indian chiefs in that area. One year, as winter began to approach, Jacob Hamblin told his son to take a certain horse, ride over to Chief Big Feather, and trade it for blankets. As the boy tied the horse to the horn of his saddle, Jacob Hamblin said, "Make a good trade."

The boy soon arrived at the Indian camp, and found Chief Big Feather. "I want to trade this horse for blankets," said the boy. "How many?" asked Chief Big Feather. "Go get the blankets, and I'll tell you," replied the boy.

The chief brought armfuls of blankets and began to put them in a pile. When the chief had put down enough blankets to trade for the horse, he asked the boy if that was enough. The boy said no and asked for more blankets. Soon there were twice as many blankets as what the horse was worth. Satisfied, the boy tied them to his horse, and started back for home.

When he arrived home, he said, "Well Dad, how's that for a good trade?" Jacob Hamblin took the blankets off the horse, and piled them into a high stack. He then split the stack in half, and told his son, "Ride back to Chief Big Feather at once with half these blankets. Tell him that Jacob Hamblin never drives an unfair bargain."

The boy rode slowly back to the reservation. When he found the chief he sheepishly said, "My father sent these blankets back." Chief Big Feather smiled and said, "I knew he would. Jacob Hamblin is an honest man."

TO HAVE INTEGRITY, we must make good values and standards our way of life. Integrity isn't something we practice just some of the time, and it isn't something we practice only when other people are watching. Integrity means choosing the right and not choosing the wrong. If a thing is right, it can and should be done; if wrong, it can and should be done without.

ABRAHAM LINCOLN (1809-1865, 16th President of the United States of America) was a man of honor and integrity. He didn't always win, and he didn't always succeed, but he was true to himself and others. He said, "I am not bound to win, but I am bound to be true. I am not bound to succeed, but I am bound to live up to the light I have. I must stand with anybody who stands right, stand with him while he is right, and part with him when he goes wrong."

HAVE YOU EVER stretched a rubber band? It always comes back to its original size and shape. What about a sweater? This is a little different. If you stretch the sweater too much it won't go back to its original shape. You can see bumps and bulges for quite a while. The trouble with stretching the truth is the same as with stretching a sweater—you can't get it back to its true shape again, although your chances are much better with the sweater.

WHAT IF SOMEONE came to you one night with a scheme that would make you rich, and all you had to do was just not do a part of your job? Would you do it? Because you weren't actively involved, would that make it all right? There was a man who lived many years ago that had to make this very choice.

This man had been a teamster for an ore company. Later he became the forwarding agent. As such, part of his responsibility was to receive the rich ore from the mine and to see that the train cars where the rich ore was stored were securely locked every night. Late one evening, two miners came to his cabin office. After a friendly greeting, one of the miners said to the agent, "If you will just forget to lock car number 16 tonight, we will pass by, and then later on we can make a small shipment ourselves. The ore is rich, it will be a big load, and we can share half the money. You run no risks."

The agent rose out of his chair, and looked out the window into the blinding snow, while the miners waited for a reply. Then after a few moments of thought and with a determined look, the agent turned to his tempters and said, "I have always had all I could eat, and all I needed to wear. I have always been able to look my employers, my fellow men, my wife and my children in the face, and I want to keep doing it. The sooner you swallow your cursed proposition and clear out, the sooner I will forget you live. There's the door."

—⚬⚬⚬—

IT IS A PRIVILEGE to work hard, and those that do work hard often find they will still have work even when others won't. Herbert N. Casson (1869-1951, British clergyman and author) said, "The slow and listless worker is the first one to be laid off. And the quick and alert worker is the first one to be given a higher position. Two-thirds of 'promotion' consists of 'motion.'

—⚬⚬⚬—

PART OF BEING honest and having integrity is doing your best when you are given an assignment. Sometimes things don't turn out the way that you would expect, but you still have a responsibility to be honest and not hide the truth. A story is told of a great king who lived a long time ago. This king was a good king. He didn't have any children, and therefore no heir to his throne. Being a wise king, he decided on a plan that would determine who would be the next king. He called all the young men in his kingdom together, and gave them some seeds. The king told them to go home, plant the seeds, and take good care of the plant, and after three months he would bring them all together again. The young man with the most beautiful plant would be the next king.

One young man took his seeds home, planted them, watered them, and took very good care of them. Yet despite several weeks worth of effort, he saw his seeds were not sprouting. Nevertheless, he was diligent and continued to take care of them.

At the end of three months, the young men in the kingdom gathered together again. All of the young men carried beautiful plants, except the one young man. In fact, he was almost too embarrassed to return to the king; however, the king required that everyone had to return and show what became of the seeds.

The king looked over the plants, all beautiful and well cared for. Finally, the king saw one empty pot and asked the young man what became of his seeds. The young man replied that he had done his best to take care of the seeds, but they never grew. The empty pot was all he had to show for his efforts.

Smiling, the king announced that this young man would become his heir. He then explained to all that he had boiled the seeds before he gave them to the young men, and none of them could have grown. This young man was the only one who was honest and had returned with the original seeds he had been given.

WE BELIEVE IN GOD because we believe there is more to life than just this life. Benjamin Franklin (1706-1790, printer, inventor, statesman) was a remarkable person. He served on the committee to help write the Declaration of Independence. He also did many other things to help promote the freedom and development of this nation. For many years he owned a print shop and was know as a printer, inventor, and philosopher. Franklin was deeply religious and had a strong belief in God. Several years before his death, he wrote his own epitaph. This is how he wanted to be remembered:

> The body of
> BENJAMIN FRANKLIN, Printer,
> Like the cover of an old book,
> its contents torn out,
> and stripped of its lettering and gilding,
> lies here food for worms;
> Yet the work itself shall not be lost,
> For it will (as he believed) appear once more
> in a new and more beautiful edition
> Corrected and amended.

THERE ARE RESPONSIBILITIES and duties that come with privileges. Look at someone who has a lot of privileges, and you will also see that they have many responsibilities. Those who seek to have privileges without also fulfilling their duties are those who are also trying to neglect their values and principles. Dwight D. Eisenhower (1890-1969, 34th President of the United States of America) said, "A people that values its privileges above its principles soon loses both."

—⁓⁓—

SCOUTS ARE AMERICANS, and with that privilege comes responsibilities. William Tyler Page (1868-1942, clerk at the U.S. House of Representatives) wrote how he felt about America. He stated it so well that the U.S. House of Representatives adopted his words as "The American Creed" on April 3, 1917.

"I believe in the United States of America as a Government of the people, by the people, for the people; whose just powers are derived from the consent of the governed; a democracy in a republic; a sovereign Nation of many sovereign States; a perfect union, one and inseparable; established upon those principles of freedom, equality, justice, and humanity for which American patriots sacrificed their lives and fortunes.

"I therefore believe it is my duty to my country to love it; to support its Constitution; to obey its laws; to respect its flag, and to defend it against all enemies."

—⁓⁓—

DOES IT MEAN MORE to you if you have to work hard for something, compared to if it were just given to you? It's a fact that the harder you work for something, the more it means to you.

Thomas Paine (1737-1809, American political philosopher) was a patriot during the American Revolution. He said, "The harder the conflict, the more glorious the triumph. What we obtain too cheap, we esteem too lightly. 'Tis dearness only that gives everything its value. Heaven knows how to put a proper price upon its goods; and it would be strange indeed, if so celestial an article as Freedom should not be highly rated."

——⚬⚬⚬——

WHAT'S MORE IMPORTANT, freedom or safety? Benjamin Franklin (1706-1790, printer, inventor, statesman) when speaking about liberty said, "They that can give up liberty to obtain a little temporary safety deserve neither their liberty nor safety."

Don't sell yourself short by giving up liberty. True safety comes by protecting freedom and not by trading it away.

——⚬⚬⚬——

THE AMERICAN FLAG represents our nation. We honor our nation by honoring the flag. You can often tell how a person feels about his country by how he treats the flag.

J. Edgar Hoover (1895-1972, director of the Federal Bureau of Investigation) stressed the importance of respecting our flag with this statement, "May we as Americans live up to our sacred trust by protecting our flag and all that it symbolizes. This is the first order of the day for every patriotic citizen."

A HERO is an ordinary person who sees a need, and is willing to sacrifice and suffer for another person who is willing but unable to do it for himself. There are many heroes around us. Many of these heroes are ordinary people who unselfishly give of themselves to provide comfort and aid to those in need.

HEROES

Men of the mountain,
Men of the plain
Who drink of the fountain
Of suffering and pain.

Men of valor
And men of might
Who live every hour
To do what is right.

Men of wisdom
And men of strength
Who cherish freedom
And guard it at length.

Men who talk
And men who do
Who show by their walk
That their word is true.

With these I care
To place my name

> But I must dare
> To live the same.
>
> RON WENDEL

SCOUTS PROMISE to do their best. Although you'll still make mistakes, or even fail, the important thing is to get up and try again.

SUCCESS

> You can't fell trees without some chips
> You can't achieve without some slips
> Unless you try you'll wonder why
> Good fortune seems to pass you by.
>
> Success is not for those who quail.
> She gives her best to those who fail,
> And then with courage twice as great
> Take issue once again with fate.
> 'Tis better far to risk a fall
> Then not to make an attempt at all.

THERE IS A STORY about General Zachary Taylor (1784-1850, 12th President of the United States of America), who became famous during the Mexican War. During one particular battle, the victory hung in the balance, and a certain enemy cannon (or battery as they used to call them) was tipping the scale against his troops. General Taylor knew something had to be done, so he called the cavalry commander and told him, "Take that battery!"

The officer answered, "We will try, sir." The general snarled back, "I don't want you to try, sir. I want you to take it."

"We will take it, or die," replied the young officer. At this, the general bellowed back, "I don't want you to die, I want you to take that battery."

Sometimes when a job needs to be done, we simply need to do it. Don't look for reasons to fail, don't make excuses about why things aren't working. Learn to be a person who makes things happen. Be someone who can turn thought into action and be a person who gets things done.

—m—

WE ALL HAVE CHALLENGES to overcome, whether it's just having a bad day, trudging through a difficult trial, or facing a serious disability. Booker T. Washington (1856-1915, American educator) said, "I have learned that success is to be measured not so much by the position that one has reached, as by the obstacle which he has over come while trying to succeed."

—m—

IT'S THE TRIALS and temptations we face that show the rest of the world what kind of person we are. It's the attitude you have when things go wrong that proves whether you're a person who is willing to work hard and try again, or one who gives up too easily. Ella Wheeler Wilcox (1850-1919, poet and journalist) inspired us to try and be among the winners when life's battles become tough.

WORTH WHILE

It is easy enough to be pleasant,
When life flows by like a song.
But the man worthwhile is one who will smile,
When everything goes dead wrong.
For the test of the heart is trouble,
And it always comes with the years,
And the smile that is worth the praises of earth
Is the smile that shines through tears.

It is easy enough to be prudent,
When nothing tempts you to stray,
When without or within no voice of sin
Is luring your soul away;
But it's only a negative virtue
Until it is tried by fire,
And the life that is worth the honor of earth
Is the one that resists desire.

By the cynic, the sad, the fallen,
Who had no strength for the strife,
The world's highway is cumbered today;
They make up the sum of life.
But the virtue that conquers passion,
And the sorrow that hides in a smile,
It is these that are worth the homage on earth
For we find them but once in a while.

———✺———

LOOK AT ANY successful person, like a great leader, inventor or businessman. In many cases they are not the strongest or the brightest individuals, but they are the ones who have learned to work the hardest. Samuel Johnson (1709-1784, British writer) said, "Great works are performed, not by strength, but by perseverance."

———✺———

ONE OF THE HARDEST lessons to learn is that we don't appreciate something until we lose it. Sometimes we take things for granted and don't realize how important they are until they are taken away from us. Here is a story about a man who took his country for granted, and then lost it.

In 1805, a man named Aaron Burr attempted to set up a new government in some of the southwestern states of the United States. When the plot was discovered, Burr and his associates were tried for conspiracy against the U.S. government. Among those convicted was a young army officer named Phillip Nolan. During his trial, Nolan was asked whether he wished to say anything to show that he had always been faithful to the U.S. Nolan replied in anger that he condemned the U.S. and said that he wished he'd never hear of the U.S. again.

Not long after, Nolan was sentenced to remain aboard a U.S. Navy ship for the rest of his life. Further, his guards were instructed that he should never again see or hear the name of his country or receive any information whatsoever concerning it. People around him were not permitted to talk about the U.S., and any newspapers that Nolan read were first read by someone else and if the paper referred to the U.S., that reference would be cut out before Nolan could read it. When the ship Nolan lived on was headed in to port, it would first meet up with an outbound ship before any sight of land, and Nolan would be transferred to the outgoing ship, forever out of sight of the U.S.

Years went by. The conditions under which he lived caused him intense anguish and sorrow. He became a changed man, and within his heart there grew an intense love for his native land. Phillip Nolan finally died. On a slip of paper that he had placed within his Bible, he had written his last request, "Bury me at sea; it had been my home and I love it. But will not someone set up a stone for my memory at Fort Adams or at Orleans, that my disgrace may not be more than I ought to bear? Say on it: In memory of Phillip Nolan, Lieutenant in the Army of the United States. He loved his country as no other man has loved her; but no man deserved less at her hands."

WORKING AT A JOB is more than just showing up in the morning, doing what you're asked to do, and then going home in the evening. You need to learn to not complain. Instead, learn to show loyalty and respect for the work that you do, and the people you work for. Elbert Hubbard (1856-1915, Author) said, "If you work for a man, then in heaven's name work for him: speak well of him and stand by the institution he represents. Remember, an ounce of loyalty is worth a pound of being a smart aleck. If you must growl, condemn, and eternally find fault, then why not resign your position? And then when you are on the outside of that institution, you can curse it to your heart's content, but as long as you are a part of the institution, do not condemn it. If you do find yourself among the complainers, you may also find that the first high wind that comes along will blow you away, and you will probably never even know why."

—∿∿—

JUST BECAUSE YOU can get away with something, and not get caught doesn't make it right. There are consequences for the choices that we make. Sometimes the consequences take years to come back to us, but they always do. Consider the following story.

Many years ago a farmer came home one evening and told his boys, "I just saw Mr. Brown today, and he wants to buy a cow. This is our chance to get rid of old Betsy. She's not that great of a cow, and if we don't milk her tonight or tomorrow morning, her udder will be enlarged and that will draw his attention. At that point I want you boys to jump in and say that Betsy is the best cow we have, and that we just couldn't possibly get rid of her. If we do this right, he'll want that old cow even more." The boys agreed to go along with the plan, and follow their father's lead in tricking Mr. Brown.

The next day Mr. Brown arrived, and sure enough everything went just as they planned. They sold the cow to Mr. Brown at an unfair price and then, after Mr. Brown left with the cow, the boys and their father laughed at what a sucker Mr. Brown had been.

What happened to Mr. Brown and the cow isn't as important as what happened to those boys. Each of those boys grew up and ended up serving time in prison. Anytime you take advantage of another person, you hurt yourself more than you actually gain. Always try to be honest in your dealings with others. It's this honesty that keeps character strong and society healthy.

MIND

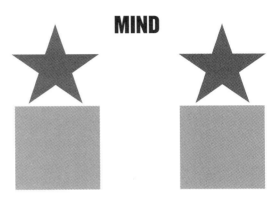

A SCOUT IS **OBEDIENT**. A SCOUT FOLLOWS THE RULES OF HIS FAMILY, SCHOOL, AND TROOP. HE OBEYS THE LAWS OF HIS COMMUNITY AND COUNTRY. IF HE THINKS THESE RULES AND LAWS ARE UNFAIR, HE TRIES TO HAVE THEM CHANGED IN AN ORDERLY MANNER RATHER THAN DISOBEYING THEM.

A SCOUT IS **CHEERFUL**. A SCOUT LOOKS FOR THE BRIGHT SIDE OF THINGS. HE CHEERFULLY DOES TASKS THAT COME HIS WAY. HE TRIES TO MAKE OTHERS HAPPY.

IN THE SCOUT OATH, a Scout promises to keep his mind mentally awake. The statesman Benjamin Disraeli (1804-1881, novelist and British prime minister) expressed it this way when he said, "Nurture your mind with great thoughts, for you will never go any higher than you think."

YOU CANNOT HIDE what kind of a person you are. The way you feel inside will sooner or later show itself on your face, through your words and by the way you act. Some things will quickly show what kind of a person you are. Remember, how a person plays a game shows something of his character, and how that person wins or loses shows all of it.

MANY OF US HAVE gifts and talents but we either do not use them, or if we do we don't use them to their fullest. Every once in a while we see someone who seems like an average person. They don't seem to have any great gifts, yet they work very hard, seem persistent, and remain very successful. Calvin Coolidge (1872-1933, 30th President of the United States of America) noticed this when he said, "Nothing in the world can take the place of persistence. Talent will not; nothing is more common than unsuccessful men with talent. Genius will not; unrewarded genius is almost a proverb. Education will not; the world is full of educated derelicts. Persistence and determination alone are omnipotent."

ANYTHING WORTHWHILE in this life requires effort. You may have the talent to be physically athletic or mentally quick, but if you wish to excel, you must sharpen that talent. A story is told of a woman who went up to a violinist after his concert and told him, "I would give half my life to be able to play as well as you do." To this the violist replied, "That is exactly what I have done." Every great talent requires sacrifice and work. To have the reward, we must pay the price and put forth the effort.

A SCOUT IS MORALLY STRAIGHT, no matter what life hands him. Sometimes two brothers can grow up in the same family, yet seem to be completely different, almost as if different winds or storms are blowing them in different directions. Each brother had to pass through the same storms of life, however, so the difference lies in the way that each man handled those storms. By being morally straight, we handle the storms of life in a way that will not injure or abuse others or ourselves. Ella Wheeler Wilcox (1850-1919, poet and journalist) wrote:

> One ship drives east,
>   and another drives west,
> With the selfsame winds that blow;
> 'Tis the set of the sails,
> And not the gales
> Which tells us the way to go.

Like the winds of the sea are
    like the ways of fate
As we voyage along through life:
'Tis the will of the soul
That decides the goal
And not the calm or strife.

—⟋𝑚⟍—

THE PAST IS SET in stone. What's been done is done, and the strongest and smartest people on earth can't bring it back or change anything that's already happened. On the other hand the future has not been written yet. It is filled with hopes and dreams. Anything can happen; anything is still possible. However, neither the past nor the future are as important as the attitude we carry with us. Ralph Waldo Emerson (1803-1882, American essayist, poet, and philosopher) said, "What lies behind us and what lies before us are small matters compared to what lies within us."

—⟋𝑚⟍—

THE SCOUT MOTTO is "Be prepared," and the best way to prepare for the future is to make good decisions today. To a large extent, the experiences you have tomorrow depend on the choices you make today. Some choices are more important than others, and some choices require more preparation because the rewards have the potential to be greater. You can tell how important a decision is by how long you will have to live with the consequences of that decision. Learn to be prepared by making good choices and good decisions.

—⁓⁓—

LEADERS HAVE vision. They know what they're doing, and they know why they're doing it—always aware of the purpose behind the plan. But nobody is born a leader. The followers who become leaders must share the leader's vision. They look for purpose and learn to understand why certain things are done. An example of a follower who showed his leadership potential can be seen in this story of Sir Christopher Wren (1632-1723, British architect).

After a big London fire, the great English architect, Sir Christopher Wren, volunteered his services to plan and superintend the building of one of the world's greatest cathedrals. He was unknown to most of the workers, and he took advantage of this and would pass among them often and watch the construction. On one occasion, he put the same question to three separate stonecutters. He simply asked them what they were doing.

One of them answered, "I am cutting this stone."

Another answered, "I am earning my three shillings per day."

But the third stood up and proudly said, "I am helping Sir Christopher Wren build this magnificent cathedral."

HABITS ARE HARD to break. Whether they are good habits or bad habits, once established, they are hard to change. If you develop good habits, this will work to your advantage and make you even stronger. Bad habits can make you a slave and bind you to their service.

An old man once remarked, "When I was a little boy, somebody gave me a cucumber in a bottle. The neck of the bottle was small, and the cucumber was large. I wondered how it got in there. Then when I was out in a garden one day, I came upon a bottle that had been slipped over a young cucumber that was still on the vine. Then I understood. The cucumber had grown while in the bottle.

"Often I see men with habits. I wonder how any strong, sensible man could be a slave to such habits. Then I remember the lesson of the cucumber, and I think that the habit most likely started while he was young, he has grown into it, and now is unable to slip out of it."

THE SCOUT MOTTO is "Be prepared." One way to be prepared is to learn to think ahead, and plan for tomorrow while it still is today. Developing your talents and skills today will result in great rewards in the future. Do things the right way now to benefit yourselves and others in times to come. As most farmers know, the time to fix a leaky roof is while the sun is out, and before the next storm arrives, and the time to mend a fence is before the cows get out, not after they are already gone. This story shows us an excellent example of what it truly means to be prepared.

Farmer White was unhappy with a man who worked for him on his farm, so he set out for the fair to hire another man. When he came to the fair, he saw farmers and their wives, dairymaids and strong young farm workers walking up and down the main throughway. Remembering he needed to hire a new farm hand, he began looking for one. He walked up to an awkward young man, and asked him, "Young fellow, what's your name?" "John," he replied. Farmer White then asked, "What do you do?" "I work on a farm," came the reply. Farmer White continued, "Do you know anything about farming?" To this, John said, "Yes sir, I know how to sleep on a windy night."

The farmer thought to himself, "I've had far too many farm hands that could sleep on any night." So the farmer went on. He walked the fair, talking to this young man and that, but none of them seemed to suit him. Later that day Farmer White ran into John again, and he asked John the same question and got the same strange answer. Yet there was something in John's honest eyes that the farmer liked, something behind what he said that interested him. So Farmer White finally said, "You are certainly a curious kind of farm hand, but come along to my farm and we'll see what you can do."

John worked away for several weeks. He was a good worker, and he worked hard, but there didn't seem to be anything exceptional about him. Then one night the wind started up. It gathered itself in gusts on the hills, and sent the clouds scurrying across the sky. It was the kind of wind that would roar through the forest, hammer against the buildings and tear at the haystacks. It woke Farmer White with a start, and he sat straight up in bed. He knew that wind was the kind of wind that would bring destruction. Many a time before, a wind like that had come and wrenched the doors off his barns, bowled over his chicken coops and scattered his hay. He didn't have a moment to lose. He jumped out of bed, and shouted for John who was sleeping in the attic. No answer. Farmer White shouted for John again, and again, no answer.

He was losing precious minutes. He didn't have time to run up to the attic and get John; instead, he ran outside to save what he could before it was too late. As he rushed out into the wild night, he expected to see everything tumbled about. Instead, he found the stable doors safely fastened, and the horses safely tethered. The windows were firmly locked, and the cattle were snug in their stalls. The haystacks were well roped, and the ropes were all well pegged. He found the pigsty secure and the chicken coop firm, and all this while the wind tore fiercely around them. Then it came to Farmer White, and he laughed out loud. He now understood how John could sleep on a windy night.

HAVE YOU EVER PRAYED to have more patience only to find that everything thing that was happening to you was making you wait more? Or did you ask for help to be more obedient only to find that you now had more temptations to disobey? Morris Adler (1870-1937, Austrian psychiatrist) said, "Our prayers are answered, not when we are given what we ask; but when we are challenged to be what we can be."

—⁕—

Have you ever had instructions and not followed them, thinking you can do just fine on your own? Then after about the second or third mistake you realize that maybe you should at least look over the instructions so you don't make any more mistakes. It is so simple to do something when you follow the instructions.

At the 1986 World's Fair in Vancouver, British Columbia, one pavilion displayed beautiful pictures on the wall. Under each picture was a caption that either explained the picture, or gave some kind of thought-provoking message. One picture captured a beautiful image of the earth from outer space, and the caption read something like this, "Too bad it didn't come with instructions."

Maybe this earth really did come with instructions, it's just that nobody wants to read and follow them. Mankind has various scriptures as well as the words of inspired men throughout the ages. If people would truly take to heart the counsels of these prophets, philosophers, and sages, they would find the instructions required to run this world.

WE ARE NOT MEANT to have all of the answers in this life. If we did have all of the answers, could we then really learn to have faith in God? The following poem shows how God is leaving the choice to us as to whether we will choose to believe in Him or not.

When in the beginning of the years,
God mixed in man the raptures and the tears
And scattered through his brain the starry stuff,
He said, "Behold! Yet this is not enough,
For I must test his spirit to make sure
That he can dare the vision and endure.

"I will withdraw my face,
Veil me in shadow for a certain space,
And leave behind only a broken clue,
A crevice where the glory shimmers through,
Some whisper from the sky,
Some footprints in the road to track me by.

"I will leave man to make the fateful guess,
Will leave him torn between the no and yes,
Leave him unresting till he rests in me.
Drawn upward by the choice that makes him free,
Leave him in tragic loneliness to choose,
With all in life to win, or all to lose."

AUTHOR UNKNOWN

HOW CAN A SCOUT perform his duty to God and his country? One way to serve is to improve yourself, and as you improve yourself, you will also find an inner peace and happiness. David O. McKay (1873-1970, American educator and religious leader) shared ten rules of happiness. They are:

1. Develop yourself by self-discipline.
2. Joy comes through creation, sorrow through destruction.
3. Do things that are hard to do.
4. Entertain uplifting thoughts.
5. Do your best this hour, and you will do better the next.
6. Be true to those who trust you.
7. Pray for wisdom, courage, and a kind heart.
8. Give heed to God's messages.
9. True friends enrich life; if you would have friends, be one.
10. Faith is the foundation of all things, including happiness.

SEVERAL YEARS AGO people used to joke when they did something wrong, and say, "The devil made me do it." Actually, the devil can't make us do anything. All he can do is to try and make the wrong look appealing. A preacher once put it this way, "God votes for me. The devil votes against me, but I cast the deciding ballot."

A SCOUT IS OBEDIENT, but how important is it to be obedient? Do rules and laws really hold us back and keep us from enjoying life? The following story illustrates how laws support our lives and make them even better.

A boy and his dad took their kite one windy day, and began to fly it. The wind was strong, and soon the kite soared higher and higher. Within just a short while, they had let out all of their line, and the kite was just a small dot in the sky. The boy, caught up in the excitement of flying the kite, asked his dad, "Isn't the string holding the kite down? And if we let go of the string, will the kite go even higher?" To this the dad replied, "No, it's just the opposite. It is the string that holds the kite up. If we let go of the string, the kite would fall to the ground and be lost."

Sometimes we look at rules and laws and even the commandments of God in the same way. We think that they are holding us back, when in truth, they are the very things that hold us up. We have a free society because of these rules and laws, and because people obey and respect the laws. Good rules and laws are there to protect people. A great danger is to think that disobeying the laws will give us more freedom. Instead, it is through disobedience that innocent people are hurt and suffer.

SOMETIMES WE don't understand words. Sometimes we think we know what a word means but then when someone asks us, we realize that we can't put our understanding into words. For example, what does it mean to believe? How would you explain a word like that to a friend?

Many years ago a missionary in Africa wanted to translate the Gospel of John into the Sango language. However, he couldn't find a word in Sango that meant "believe." He took the problem to a native Christian. The man thought for a few minutes and then suggested, "Doesn't it mean to 'hear in my heart'?"

SOMETIMES WE might wish we were as rich as our neighbor or had the same nice clothes as a friend. Other times we wish we were smarter or more talented. One secret for being unhappy is to always compare ourselves to someone else. It won't matter how talented, or smart or wealthy we are, we'll always wish we were something different. On the other hand, one secret to being happy is to learn to be content with who we are and what we have. If there is something about ourselves that we don't like, then change what we don't like, and make ourselves better people. If there is something that we don't have that we really want, then we should work and save and earn it.

There are too many people who are talented, smart, and wealthy, yet remain unhappy. They are too busy looking at what everyone else has, and measuring that against what they don't have. This life is often compared to a race, but the difference is that we don't race against others—we only race against ourselves. A happy person learns to be happy with what they have, and to let others be happy with what they have. A happy person learns to be better today than he was yesterday. In that way, that person is winning the race.

—⚮—

A SCOUT IS CHEERFUL. As we get dressed every morning, we always need to remember to put on a smile along with our clothes. We're never really fully dressed until we put on a smile. Besides, a smile increases our face value.

—⚮—

IT TAKES DETERMINATION to never give up. True determination comes from within your heart. It is a spirit of faith and trust that gives you a hope and belief that you can accomplish what you need to do. Jim Irwin (1930-1991, Air Force pilot, astronaut) was a very determined man.

There have only been a dozen astronauts that walked on the moon and Jim Irwin was one of them. But it wasn't the fact that he had been to the moon that made him great. He was great because of the way he lived. Jim Irwin liked to meet with the youth and talk to them. He would tell them to reach for their dreams, and to aim high—no matter how difficult, and no matter what obstacles were in their way. And Jim Irwin was qualified to say that.

Because of what he had gone through in his life, Jim Irwin had learned not to accept defeat, even though the odds were against him. You see, as a young pilot, his plane crashed, and though he survived, the accident smashed both of his legs. The doctors said that he would never walk again, and that he definitely would never fly again. He would be confined to a wheelchair or crutches for the rest of his life. But that did not stop Jim Irwin. He defied the odds because he would not accept defeat. He did walk again, and eventually flew again. Then, not only did he fly again, but also became an astronaut and went to the moon.

A PERSON MUST BE brave to try something new, or to work on something that they are not good at until they become good at it. Winston Churchill (1874-1965, British politician and prime minister) said, "Courage is the first of human qualities because it is the quality which guarantees all the others."

This is especially true if we wish to improve ourselves. It takes courage to work on a weakness and make it strong. It takes courage to keep trying to be better at something. An example of this can be seen in the life of Benjamin Franklin (1706-1790, printer, inventor and statesman). He made a list of qualities and attributes that he wanted to make a part of his life. Then each week he would select one and focus on that quality. He would practice it and work on it and make it a part of his character.

IT IS THE TRIALS and the hardships we must go through that bring out the worst in some, and the best in others.

The effort to endure these trials and hardships makes us strong, just like the eagles in this poem.

Storms Bring Out the Eagles
But the Little Birds Take Cover

When the "storms of life" gather darkly ahead,
I think of these wonderful words I once read
And I say to myself as "threatening clouds" hover
Don't "fold up your wings" and "run for cover"
But like the eagle "spread wide your wings"
and "soar far above" the trouble life brings,
For the eagle knows that the higher he flies
The more tranquil and brighter become the skies . . .
And there is nothing in life God ever asks us to bear
That we can't soar above "On the Wings of Prayer,"
And in looking back over the "storm you passed
    through"
You'll find you gained strength and new courage, too,
For in facing "life's storms" with an eagle's wings
You can fly far above earth's small, petty things.

Helen Steiner Rice
(1900-1981, Poet, author)

It takes courage to face your fears; but it also takes courage to face pain. Some people face pain every day and still perform at their very best. It takes a brave person to be successful, even though they are suffering and in great pain.

Walter Johnson (1887-1946, pitcher for the Washington

Senators) was one of the greatest pitchers in the history of baseball. Before one crucial game where he was scheduled to pitch, his arm was painfully sore. His manager, Clark Griffith, told him, "Try one inning, and if your arm gives you trouble, I'll take you out." After the first inning, Johnson's arm still pained him, but he said he would try another. After the second inning, his arm still hurt, but he tried another inning. This continued throughout the game, and by the end of the ninth inning and in out-and-out agony, Walter Johnson pitched the only no-hitter in his twenty-year career.

IT'S IMPORTANT to learn how to make wise decisions, and to have the courage to make big decisions rather than avoid them.

Andrew Jackson (1767-1845, 7th President of the United States of America) said, "Take time to deliberate; but when the time for action arrives, stop thinking and go in."

William Feather (1889-1981, author and publisher) said, "Conditions are never just right. People who delay action until all factors are favorable do nothing."

And finally, David Lloyd George (1863-1945, British statesman) said, "Don't be afraid to take a big step if one is indicated. You can't cross a chasm in two small jumps."

It doesn't matter how many times you fall down as long as you get back up each time. The ability to get back up is called persistence. Those who learn to make persistence a part of their character will eventually succeed, while those who don't simply won't. Another clever way to say it is that failure is the path of least persistence.

Failure is not falling down, but staying down. Every time you get back up, you haven't failed. Every time you make one more try, or give it one more effort, you haven't failed.

***

HOW DANGEROUS is a bad habit? You may not think much of it right now, but if you make it a part of your life, you will regret it. It may not be tomorrow, it may not even be next year, but that fateful day will come. We should always try to improve ourselves and get rid of our bad habits. If not, we may end up like the forgotten wedge, described in this story by Samuel T. Whitman.

The ice storm wasn't generally destructive. True, a few wires came down and there was a sudden jump in accidents along the highway. Walking out of doors became unpleasant and difficult. It was disagreeable weather, but it was not serious. Normally, the big walnut tree could easily have borne the weight that formed on its spreading limbs. It was the iron wedge in its heart that caused the damage.

The story of the iron wedge began years ago when the white-haired farmer was a lad on his father's homestead. The sawmill had then only recently been moved from the valley and the settlers were still finding tools and odd pieces of equipment scattered about.

On this particular day, it was a faller's wedge—wide, flat and heavy, a foot or more long, and splayed from mighty poundings. The path from the south pasture did not pass the woodshed; and, because he was already late for dinner, the lad laid the wedge between the limbs of the young walnut tree his father had planted near the front gate. He would take the wedge to the shed right after dinner, or sometime when he was going that way.

He truly meant to, but he never did. It was there between the limbs, a little tight, when he attained his manhood. It was there, now firmly gripped, when he married and took over his father's farm. It was half grown over on the day the threshing crew ate dinner under the tree. Grown in and healed over, the wedge was still in the tree when the winter ice storm came.

In the chill silence of that wintry night, with the mist like rain sitting down and freezing where it fell, one of the three major limbs split away from the trunk and crashed to the ground. This so unbalanced the remainder of the top that it, too, split apart and went down. When the storm was over, not a twig of the once-proud tree remained.

Early the next morning, the farmer went out to mourn his loss. "Wouldn't have had that happen for a thousand dollars," he said. "Prettiest tree in the valley, that was."

Then his eyes caught sight of something in the splintered ruin. "The wedge," he muttered reproachfully. "The wedge I found in the south pasture." A glance told him why the tree had fallen. Growing edge-up in the trunk, the wedge had prevented the limb fibers from knitting together, as they should.

LEARN TO THINK for yourself, and don't follow the crowd. Just because everyone else is doing it, doesn't mean that you need to. Or just because it has always been done that way doesn't mean that it is the right way. In many cases we need to follow the rules that have been set so that we maintain order within our society. On the other hand, there are rules that had a reason many years ago when they were first made, but they have lost their purpose as time has passed. Sam Walter Foss (1858-1911, poet, journalist, and publisher) wrote a poem that illustrates the kind of trouble we get into when we don't learn to think for ourselves.

> One day through the primeval wood
> A calf walked home as good calves should;
> But made a trail all bent askew,
> A crooked trail as all calves do.

> Since then three hundred years have fled,
> And I infer the calf is dead.
> But still he left behind his trail,
> And thereby hangs my moral tale.
> The trail was taken up next day
> By a lone dog that passed that way;
> And then a wise bellwether sheep
> Pursed the trail o'er hill and glade
> Through those old woods a path was made.
> And many men wound in and out
> And dodged and turned and bent about
> And uttered words of righteous wrath

Because 'twas such a crooked path.
But still they followed—do not laugh—
The first migrations of that calf,
And through this winding wood-way stalked
Because he wobbled when he walked.

The forest path became a lane
That bent and turned and turned again;
This crooked lane became a road,
Where many a poor horse with his load
Toiled on beneath the burning sun
And traveled some three miles in one.
And thus a century and a half
They trod the footsteps of that calf.

.

The years passed on in swiftness fleet,
The road became a village street;
And thus, before men were aware,
A city's crowded thoroughfare.
And soon the central street was this
Of a renowned metropolis;
And man two centuries and a half
Trod in the footsteps of that calf.

Each day a hundred thousand rout
Followed this zigzag calf about
And o'er this crooked journey went
The traffic of a continent.
A hundred thousand men were led
By one calf near three centuries dead.

They followed still his crooked way,
And lost one hundred years a day;
For thus such reverence is lent
To well-established precedent.

—⁓—

WE ALL HAVE GIFTS and talents, and it is each person's duty to use them. Remember, if you do not use them, you will lose them. Charles Darwin (1809-1882, British scientist) often said that after he had finished his scientific work, he would finally be able to settle down and enjoy life. He thought that he would finally be able to enjoy poetry, music and art. However, after never taking the time to enjoy them earlier in his life, he sadly discovered that these things did not strike a response in his being when he did have the time. Later he said, "It is too late now because I have allowed these parts of my being to atrophy."

—⁓—

THOSE WHO FAIL to prepare are preparing to fail. The story is told of a young boy who would not go to school. Instead, he would sit on the curb and say, "I'm just as smart as they are. I don't need any schooling." At first, he was right. He was just as smart as any other kid. But day after day, he used this excuse, and as the years came and went he fell behind. Finally, when it came time for him to graduate, and while all his friends received their diplomas, he didn't and for many years after that, he paid a dear price for being behind.

The story continues to a young boy who never went to church on Sunday. Instead, he would sit on the curb and say, "I'm just as good as they are. I don't need any religion." At first, he was right. He was just as good as any other kid. But week after week he used this excuse, and as the years came and went, he never learned the scriptures or heard the stories that could make him a better person. And for many years after that he paid a dear price for being behind.

—⚋—

A SCOUT TAKES AN oath to do his duty to God and his country. Did you know that before a doctor begins to practice medicine he takes an oath to always use his skills to try and save lives? Soldiers take an oath to defend our freedoms, and even the President of the United States takes an oath to uphold the Constitution and protect the liberty of this nation.

This is nothing new. In ancient Greece, when a young man turned seventeen, he took an oath to defend his city, obey the laws, and never bring disgrace by an act of dishonesty or cowardice.

An oath is a promise that we make, and that we try to keep with all our hearts. Always try to live so that those around you know you have taken the Scout oath, and made it a part of your life.

BODY

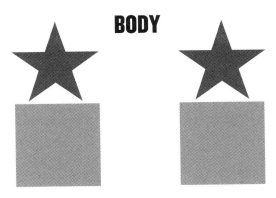

A SCOUT IS **THRIFTY**. A SCOUT WORKS TO PAY HIS WAY AND TO HELP OTHERS. HE SAVES FOR THE FUTURE. HE PROTECTS AND CONSERVES NATURAL RESOURCES. HE CAREFULLY USES TIME AND PROPERTY.

A SCOUT IS **CLEAN**. A SCOUT KEEPS HIS BODY AND MIND FIT AND CLEAN. HE ADMIRES THOSE WHO BELIEVE IN LIVING BY THESE SAME IDEALS. HE HELPS KEEP HIS HOME AND COMMUNITY CLEAN.

A SCOUT IS CLEAN—both in his speech and his thoughts.

How important is it to keep your thoughts pure and clean? Negative influences come from everywhere these days, from movies to video games to magazines. Disguised as popular or trendy, this filth makes it difficult to keep clean. Yet it is important that we make the decision within ourselves to be clean and keep our minds out of the gutter. If you put a drop of clean water into a cup of sewage, the drop of water will not change the sewage—you still have a cup of sewage. Yet if you switch it around and put a drop of sewage in a cup of clean water, that single drop changes the cup of clean water into a cup of sewage. In other words, if you play in filth, you will come away dirty. If you even just dabble in dirt, you will still come away dirty. Make the choice to be clean.

THE SCOUT OATH starts like this, "On my honor I will do my best . . ." We all need to learn to do our best all the time and in everything we do. Sometimes we think that just doing good enough is enough, and we justify ourselves by saying, "So I missed a couple of problems on the test but I still got a high score. Isn't that good enough?" If you could have done better, then even a 99.9 percent isn't good enough. In fact, there are some things where anything short of 100 percent isn't good enough. Consider the following statistics.

Even with a reliability of 99.9 percent we would still have:

1 hour of unsafe drinking water every month
2,000 unsafe airline landings per day, more
     than one a minute
16,000 lost pieces of mail by the U.S. Postal
     Service every hour
20,000 incorrect drug prescriptions each year
500 incorrect surgical operations every week
50 newborn babies dropped at birth by
     doctors every day
22,000 checks deducted from the wrong bank
     accounts every hour
32,000 missed heartbeats per person per year

Would you be willing to risk your life and safety, or the life and safety of others just because 99.9 percent should be good enough?

—m—

MOST PEOPLE equate success with how much money they have. However, wealth doesn't always measure a person's success. There are things to strive for in this world that don't come with a price tag, such as education, integrity, love, and happiness. It is better to have learning than gold, but it is even better to have a clean heart than either.

—〰—

THE PERSON you are on the inside is your true self. How you think and feel when you are all alone say more about what kind of a person you are than anything anybody else could say. The ancient Chinese philosopher Confucius (551-479 B.C., Chinese philosopher and educator) said, "Heaven will be inherited by every man who has heaven in his soul.

—〰—

OFTEN IT IS GOOD to be quick, especially in sports. The slow player ends up losing in a competitive match. However, life isn't always competitive. There are times when it is good to be slow. In fact, being slow at the right time can save a lot of trouble and pain. When might such a time be? A Chinese proverb explains, "If you are patient in one moment of anger, you will escape a hundred days of sorrow."

—〰—

WE ALL MAKE MISTAKES. We all say or do things that sooner or later we come to regret. Here are some things that we will never be sorry for.

Thinking before acting,
Hearing before judging,
Forgiving your enemies,
Being candid and frank,
Helping a fallen brother,
Being honest in business,

Thinking before speaking,
Being loyal to your church,
Standing by your principles,
Stopping your ears to gossip,
Bridling a slanderous tongue,
Harboring only pure thoughts,
Sympathizing with the afflicted,
Being courteous and kind to all.

AUTHOR UNKNOWN

THEODORE ROOSEVELT (1858-1919, 26th President of the United States) became president of the United States when William McKinley was assassinated. Not only was Roosevelt an energetic and active outdoorsman, but he was also a scholar, cowboy, soldier, conservationist, and statesman. Roosevelt did what he thought was right, even if it meant standing against other powers that pushed against him. Roosevelt demonstrated this resolve when he took steps to protect our national forests when certain lumber companies used the forests for their own selfish interests. He stood against big businesses that were taking advantage of the ordinary citizens. He wanted a "square deal, no more and no less," so that people would be treated fairly by big businesses. During his term in office, President Roosevelt won the Nobel Peace Prize for helping to end the Russo-Japanese War.

You would think that a person like this started out with everything, but that's not true. Roosevelt started out as a sickly young man who suffered from asthma and poor eyesight. He had a weak body, and his father once said that his son had a mind that could succeed, but not the body to do it. This didn't stop young Roosevelt. He exercised and went on long walks as a youth, building up his strength and stamina. Roosevelt's determination to achieve physical fitness and moral strength allowed him to have a very active life as an adult.

WE FACE MANY choices. We can't have everything, so we need to set priorities, and then make choices based on these priorities. By giving up things of less importance, we can have something of greater importance. A young man who wants a brand new bike will gladly give up his trips to the candy store, and by saving up his money the young man will find that it quickly adds up to the right amount for a bike. On the other hand, the dollars that were meant for the bike can quickly disappear when used for candy and pop.

The greatest cause of a person's unhappiness is that they trade what they want most for something they want right now. While this is true for money, it is also true for school, sports, and even careers. In fact, some of the most important things in this life will require sacrifices. Those who are willing to make the sacrifices will attain the corresponding rewards.

WOULD YOU be willing to exchange your honor for money or power? Some people have done just about anything for wealth, even bringing harm to friends or family. It is sad indeed when possessions become more important than relationships. Such was the case with the Great Wall of China.

The Great Wall of China was built to keep invaders from the north from coming down and attacking the southern provinces and villages of China. The construction was started in 200 B.C. and the massive wall was built in sections. Over the centuries, these sections joined together until they formed one continuous wall, stretching for over 4,500 miles. With an average height of 25 feet and an average width of 19 feet, the wall is well suited for defending those inside. In fact, it is said that no army who directly attacked the wall ever penetrated it, not with stones, arrows, or swords. Yet enemy armies made it over and through the mighty wall several times throughout history. How? Because of the treachery and greed of people inside—rulers, magistrates, guards, or captains that should have been protecting their own people, but instead allowed attacking armies to cross over from the north and cause much trouble. As we strive to build our own mighty walls to keep bad influences out, take care not to allow greed or dishonesty to get the better of us, or we can lose the very battles we're trying to fight.

THE "COUCH POTATO" does one thing really well—he sits. He misses out on a lot of other great things in life, but at least he can sit well. On the other hand, the person that learns to use his mind becomes successful. It doesn't matter if you're talking about school or sports; you have to think about what you're doing if you really want to be good. In other words:

> We have two ends with a common link,
> With one we sit, and with one we think.
> Success depends on which you choose,
> Heads you win; tails you lose.

AUTHOR UNKNOWN

HAVE YOU EVER TRIED to hammer in a bent nail? Even if you straighten it out before you try to reuse it, the nail still bends very easily. Only a new, straight nail will provide the best results. A carpenter beginning a new project always starts with the best materials he can find—nails, tools, and wood. In the hands of a skilled carpenter, these materials will be used to create a beautiful table or a cabinet. Remember the lesson from the carpenter; nothing beautiful can be carved from a rotten piece of wood.

Your character is the material you're using to build your life. Twenty years from now, you will begin to see the product you are building. The question to ask yourself is this: "Is the wood you're using now good wood or rotten wood?"

DO LITTLE THINGS matter? Every big thing in life is made of the little things that lead up to it. Kingdoms have been lost because the tide turned in a single but important battle.

And important battles have been lost because a crucial message never made it to the general. And why didn't that message get there? It could have been something as simple as a horse losing its shoe.

> For the sake of a nail, a shoe was lost,
> For the sake of a shoe, a horse was lost,
> For the sake of a horse, a message was lost,
> For the sake of a message, a kingdom was lost.

In today's world, we could also say:

> For the sake of a missed assignment,
>   the grade was bad,
> For the sake of a bad grade,
>   the class was failed,
> For the sake of a failed class,
>   the GPA was poor,
> For the sake of a poor GPA,
>   the college denied entrance.
> So, do little things matter?
>   You bet they do.

A BOY WAS RIDING in a truck with his grandfather one day. As they were driving around the edge of a field, the truck hit a slippery part of the dirt road and slid into a muddy ditch. The boy was a little scared, but the grandfather calmly said, "Watch this." He then proceeded to carefully and meticulously coax the truck out of the ditch. Impressed with the driving skills of his grandfather, and at the same time amazed at what he had just seen, the boy said to his grandfather, "I'll bet you can't do that again." To this, the grandfather replied, "I don't have to, I may have been unlucky enough to end up in that ditch the first time, but I'm not stupid enough to purposely put myself there a second time."

SOMETIMES A YOUNG person will think that it's no big deal to get in trouble with the law. Some may say, "The judge will let you off easy if it's your first offense, so you really have nothing to lose." However, that's not true. If you are convicted of a felony, even if you don't go to jail, you still lose a lot. Consider this:

A student was arrested and convicted for possession of a controlled substance, which is a felony. Since the amount was small, and it was a first time offense, the judge gave the young man a suspended sentence. The penalty seemed light, so the student turned to his lawyer and asked, "It doesn't seem like a big deal, so what did I really lose?"

The lawyer replied, "You've lost much more than you think. You have lost the right to vote, to run for office, or to even own a gun. In most states you cannot work for a city, county, or state government. You also cannot get a job where you have to be bonded or licensed. This means that you have lost the opportunity to be licensed as a doctor, dentist, pharmacist, physical therapist, lawyer, engineer, architect, realtor, certified public accountant, private detective, stockbroker, or even a funeral director. To be convicted of a felony is a serious offense. Even if you don't go to jail, you have limited your opportunities for the rest of your life."

———※———

IF YOU WERE to choose between saving your life and saving your wealth, which would you choose? This is a question of priorities, and the answer seems obvious; yet some people get so caught up with riches and wealth that they forget what is really important. This story by Matthew Cowley (1897-1953, American religious leader) shows that choosing wealth above all else can have serious results.

Many years ago in New Zealand, a destructive flood caused 22 foreigners to drown. They were among a work crew constructing a railway line. There were also a large number of young natives working on that same line, but not one of them lost their lives. Upon inquiry, one of the survivors was asked why none of the natives lost their lives while so many of the others had. He said, "The others ran for their money, we ran for our lives."

———※———

ONE ASPECT of being thrifty is to be happy with what you have. It is good to have goals and to work and improve your life, but at the same time you need to find satisfaction in what you have done and where you are. Those who always want more are never satisfied. Those who always want more never feel the joy of being content. We need to learn to control our desire to always want, and be happy with what we have. Socrates (469-399 B.C., Greek philosopher) said, "He is the richest who is content with the least."

————⚬————

A SCOUT IS CLEAN in his speech. When we talk with other people, it's like going on a walk through their mind, and as we listen to others, we let them walk through our minds. When we are with friends and people we like, that walk is fun and enjoyable. We like it when they listen to us, and we love listening to them. Mahatma Gandhi (1869-1948, political leader and philosopher from India) said, "I will not let anyone walk through my mind with dirty feet." We should enjoy the good walks with people, but work hard to keep out those with dirty feet.

————⚬————

SPOILED MILK tastes terrible, but it didn't start out that way. The same is true of moldy bread; it tastes awful, but it doesn't start out that way either. Fresh milk tastes wonderful, and newly baked bread is delicious. People are much the same way—as youth, our lives start out clean and good. James Allen (1864-1912, American writer) said, "Out of a clean heart comes a clean life and a clean body. Out of a defiled mind proceeds a defiled life and corrupt body. Thought is the fount of action, life and manifestation; make the fountain pure, and all will be pure."

MANY THINK that the secret to being rich is to gain a lot of money, but that is not all of it. There are many people with a lot of money, yet they end up worse off than before they had the riches. It's not the money that makes you rich so much as it is how you handle it while you have it. Whether you earn a little money or a lot, the secret to being wealthy is learning to save your money. Benjamin Franklin (1706-1790, printer, inventor, and statesman) said, "If you would be wealthy, think of saving as well as getting."

THE THINGS of real worth don't have dollar signs on them. Real wealth is measured with hours and minutes. Often we measure how important a person is by how much money they have. Instead we should measure a person by how much time they give. Those that trade just their time for money are very poor indeed.

> The real measure of wealth
> is how much you'd be worth
> if you lost all of your money.
> AUTHOR UNKNOWN

WE CAN PRACTICE being thrifty in many areas, not just where money is concerned. A good Scout practices conservation of natural resources—land, and water. He tries to protect nature from waste and destruction whenever possible. Many North American Indian nations also held nature in high regard. They took care of the land, not only because it was their home, but also because they knew their lives depended on careful use of resources, and making sure the land could renew itself. Even today, our lives depend on caring for the land, but sometimes we aren't very careful. The Cree Indians have the following expression:

> Only when the last tree has died,
> and the last river has been poisoned,
> and the last fish has been caught,
> will we realize, we cannot eat money.

IF YOU'VE EVER seen a wanted poster then you know they are made up of a picture, a reward, and a description. The description tells what to look for so that we will recognize the person. But it's not just bad people that get the wanted posters. Many times a store or business will put a wanted poster up when they need to hire a new employee. This kind of a poster doesn't have a picture or a reward, but it still gives a description that tells everybody what qualities the employer is looking for. Almost a hundred years ago, Frank Crane (1861-1928, American clergyman and journalist) wrote up a kind of "Help Wanted" list, describing the type of boy that any school, church, home, or community would like to have around. A Scout strives to be just like the boy being advertised.

BOY WANTED

A boy who stands straight, sits straight, acts straight, and talks straight.

A boy who listens carefully when spoken to, who asks questions when he does not understand, and does not ask questions about things that are none of his business.

A boy whose fingernails are not in mourning, whose ears are clean, whose shoes are polished, whose clothes are brushed, whose hair is combed, and whose teeth are well cared for.

A boy who moves quickly and makes as little noise about it as possible.

A boy who whistles in the street but not where he ought to keep still.

A boy who looks cheerful, has a ready smile for everybody, and never sulks.

A boy who is polite to every man and respectful to every woman and girl.

A boy who does not smoke and has no desire to learn how.

A boy who never bullies other boys or allows boys to bully him.

A boy who, when he does not know a thing, says, "I do not know"; and when he has made a mistake says, "I'm sorry"; and, when requested to do anything, immediately says, "I'll try."

A boy who looks you right in the eye and tells the truth every time.

A boy who would rather lose his job or be
   expelled from school than tell a lie or be a cad.

A boy who is more eager to know how to speak
   good English than to talk slang.

A boy who does not want to be "smart" nor in
   any wise attract attention.

A boy who is eager to read good, wholesome books.

A boy whom other boys like.

A boy who is perfectly at ease in the company
   of respectable girls.

A boy who is not a goody-goody, a prig, or a
   little Pharisee, but just healthy, happy, and
   full of life.

A boy who is not sorry for himself and not for
   ever thinking and talking about himself.

A boy who is friendly with his mother and
   more intimate with her than with anyone else.

A boy who makes you feel good when he is
   around.

This boy is wanted everywhere. The family wants him,
the school wants him, the office wants him, the boys and
girls want him, and all creation wants him.

THERE IS NO SECRET to practicing thrift and gaining wealth—
simply spend less than you make. In today's world, it is too
easy to buy cars, stereos, furniture, and clothing on credit. In
only a little time, people can end up owing more money than

they make. Charles Dickens (1812-1870, British novelist) wrote, "Annual income 20 pounds, annual expenditure 19 pounds, result happiness. Annual income 20 pounds, annual expenditure 21 pounds, result misery." One secret of financial unhappiness is to carry a lot of debt.

—⚜—

PART OF BEING thrifty is preparing for the future, and if we prepare for things that are expected, we will be better prepared for the unexpected. The story of the Ant and the Grasshopper shows us the wisdom of planning ahead.

In a field one summer's day, a Grasshopper hopped about, chirping and singing to his heart's content. An Ant passed by, struggling with an ear of corn.

"Why not come and chat with me," said the Grasshopper, "instead of toiling and moiling in that way?"

"I am helping to lay up food for the winter," said the Ant, "and recommend you to do the same."

"Why bother about winter?" said the Grasshopper. "We have got plenty of food at present." But the Ant went on his way and continued to toil. When the winter came, the Grasshopper had no food and found himself dying of hunger, while he saw the ants feasting every day on corn and grain from the stores they had collected in the summer. Only then did the Grasshopper realize that it is best to prepare ahead for the days of necessity.

A scout is morally clean, and being clean is a choice he must make. It isn't something that happens all by itself. He either chooses to be clean, or he chooses not to. If he chooses to be clean, he must keep filthy and corrupt things out of his life.

All the water in the world,
However hard it tried,
Could never sink the smallest ship
Unless it got inside.

All the evil in the world,
The blackest kind of sin
Could never hurt you one least bit,
Unless you let it in.

AUTHOR UNKNOWN

THERE IS A LOT of good in the world. There are good people to meet and associate with, wonderful places to go, and exciting things to do. Our lives are full of opportunities, and we should do all within our power to take advantage of these opportunities in ways that are beneficial to everyone. At the same time, there are people, places, and opportunities that are not wholesome and uplifting. These things can soil our hearts, our minds, and our souls. A Scout needs to learn to enjoy the good without touching the bad. Learn to enjoy the roses without being pricked by their thorns.

SPIRIT

A SCOUT IS **BRAVE**. A SCOUT CAN FACE DANGER EVEN IF HE IS AFRAID. HE HAS THE COURAGE TO STAND FOR WHAT HE THINKS IS RIGHT EVEN IF OTHERS LAUGH AT HIM OR THREATEN HIM.

A SCOUT IS **REVERENT**. A SCOUT IS REVERENT TOWARD GOD. HE IS FAITHFUL IN HIS RELIGIOUS DUTIES. HE RESPECTS THE BELIEFS OF OTHERS.

A SCOUT gives his best no matter what the situation. Sometimes it's not hard to do our best, but other times it seems as if everything is working against us. Some of us have personal difficulties or challenges, yet the goal is to still the same, to always do our best. The story of Michael J. Dowling illustrates that people can present their best even when the challenges seem overwhelming.

Michael J. Dowling was a young man of 14 when he fell off of the back of a wagon during a blizzard. By the time his parents found him, he was severely frostbitten. His right leg was amputated almost to the hip; his left leg above the knee; his right arm was amputated as was his left hand. It seems like Michael Dowling wouldn't have much of a future, but he was determined to get an education and be successful. He went to the board of county commissioners and told them that if they would educate him, he would pay back every penny. They agreed, and he received his education, then repaid the debt. He worked hard in his career and eventually became president of one of the largest banks in the city. Michael Dowling also married and had five children.

During World War I, Michael Dowling traveled to Europe to visit wounded American soldiers. On one occasion, he stayed in a large London hotel and gave a speech to some injured servicemen. As he stood on a balcony overlooking several hundred soldiers sitting in their wheelchairs, he started to tell them how fortunate they were. The fact that one had lost an eye, and another had lost an arm were no grounds for complaint. He continued talking this way, and within a few minutes the soldiers became angry and started to boo him. He then walked over to the stairway and started down the stairs toward the lobby. Michael Dowling continued telling them how fortunate they were, and they continued to boo him. Partway down the stairs, he sat down and removed his artificial right leg. At this point the soldiers calmed down a little, but they still resented his remarks. Michael Dowling then took off his artificial left leg, and the hall quieted immediately. Next, he took off his right arm, and finally removed his left hand. The soldiers then understood how fortunate they were.

We have little control over the gifts life gives us. We have even less control over the challenges we each must face. However, we have complete control over our attitude and how we decide to handle the hardships we must endure.

—∽—

PERSISTENCE and determination don't eliminate problems or mistakes in our lives. Instead, it means that as the problems come, we face them and work through them. We can turn our failures into successes, and win in whatever struggles we must face. Rulon B. Stanfield said it this way:

> It matters little if you try and fail,
> And fail and try again.
> But it matters much if you try and fail,
> And then fail to try again.

—◦m◦—

A Scout is brave, and a person with courage strengthens others. This brave person also finds that others quickly come to stand by him and support the cause. One person with courage often makes a majority.

—◦m◦—

NOTHING IN THIS life comes easy, and the things in life that offer the greatest rewards also require the greatest efforts. It is through hard work, determination, and persistence that victories are won and character is built. The following poem compares trees with men, and shows they both need to suffer a little to become strong.

GOOD TIMBER

The tree that never had to fight
For sun and sky and air and light;
That stood out in the open plain
And always got its share of rain
Never became a forest king,
But lived and died a scrubby thing.

The man who never had to toil
By hand or mind mid life's turmoil;
Who never had to win his share
Of sun and sky and light and air
Never became a manly man,
But lived and died as he began.

Good timber does not grow in ease
The stronger the wind, the tougher the trees;
The further the sky, the greater the length,
The more the storm, the more the strength;
By sun and cold, by rains and snows
In tree or man, good timber grows.

And where thickest stands the forest growth
We find the patriarchs of both
And they hold council with the stars
Whose broken branches show the scars
Of many winds and much strife,
This is the common law of life.

AUTHOR UNKNOWN

—〰—

A SCOUT IS REVERENT. One way to show reverence to God is by showing respect to his name and not using it in vain. It's a lesson that George Washington (1732-1799, 1st President of the United States of America) tried to teach his men.

While General George Washington was the commander-in-chief during the American Revolution, he issued an order against the use of profanity. In particular, he did not like to hear his men use the name of God in vain. Here is General Washington's order as quoted by Thayer:

"Many and frequent orders have been issued against the unmeaning and abominable custom of swearing, notwithstanding which, with much regret, the General observes that it prevails if possible, more than ever. His feelings are continually wounded by the oaths and imprecations of the soldiers, whenever he is in hearing of them. The name of that Being from whose bountiful goodness we are permitted to exist and enjoy the comforts of life is incessantly imprecated and profaned in a manner as wanton as it is shocking. For the sake, therefore of religion, decency, and order, the General hopes and trusts that officers of every rank will use their influence and authority to check a vice which is as unprincipled as it is wicked and shameful. If officers would make it an inviolable rule to reprimand, and if that won't do, to punish soldiers for an offense of this kind, it would not fail of having the desired effect."

FAITH IS A SECURE belief in God and a trusting acceptance of God's will. Those who choose to have faith are brave and courageous, while those who don't have that faith or trust in God are afraid. The following poem shows how fear and faith seem to travel together, though "they are as different as night and day."

FEAR AND FAITH
Where there's fear, there's also faith
For they travel side by side.
And they'll be found in perilous places,
Be it a storm, strong wind or high tide.

Yes, where there's fear, there's also faith
Though not in the same man do they abide;
They are as different as night and day
Though they travel side by side.

'Tis in the heart where true battles are fought
And faith and fear are foes;
The conquerors, with courage, live by faith
While the fearful live in woes.

Show me fear and I'll show you faith
Who through death's door must enter in:
One fears what lies beyond,
The other believes it opens to him.

And those who pass through daily perils
Have learned in God to confide;
Fear destroys while faith builds the soul
Though they travel side by side.

RON WENDEL

TRUE COURAGE is when you can face the unknown and not be afraid. Putting our trust in God is like taking an outstretched hand and willingly walk unafraid through the darkness and all its unknowns.

Shortly after Great Britain declared war against Nazi Germany in 1939, the king broadcast a message of encouragement to the British Empire. In that speech he quoted from a dialogue between a man and the Keeper of the Gate of the Year:

"I said to the man who stood at the gate of the year, 'Give me a light that I may tread safely into the unknown,' and he replied, 'Go out into the darkness, and put your hand in the hand of God. That shall be to you better than a light, and safer than the known way.'"

WHAT DOES IT MEAN to be sincere? If our words are not honest and sincere then they really don't mean a thing. Sincerity is especially important during prayer. William Shakespeare (1564-1616, poet and playwright) penned these words:

> My words fly up,
> My thoughts remain below
> Words without thoughts
> Never to heaven go.

—⁓—

HOW IMPORTANT is Christianity to its followers? Could it be more important than anything purchased with money or gold? As Patrick Henry (1736-1799, lawyer and patriot) approached the end of his life he said, "I have disposed of all my property to my family. There is one more thing I wish I could give them, and that is the Christian religion. If they had that and I had not given them one cent, they would be rich."

—⁓—

PART OF A SCOUT'S duty to God is to learn of Him and know Him. But how can we learn about God? Consider the following story:

A young lady bought and read a book. When she finished, she laid it aside, and made a mental note that it was the dullest book she had ever read. Not long after that, she met a young man, and in the course of time their friendship ripened into love. Then one night she said, "I have a book at my home that was written by a man whose name is exactly like yours. Isn't that a coincidence?" Upon learning the name of the book, the young man told her that he had written that book.

That very night, when the young lady returned home, she took the book down from the shelf and reread it from beginning to end. This time she found it to be the most interesting book she had ever read. Why the difference? It was because this time she knew and loved the author. And so it is with reading the holy scriptures—you will enjoy them more as you learn to know and love the author.

TAKE A STAND for right, for truth, for freedom and for justice. Don't be afraid to stand up for what you believe in, and you'll find you won't stand alone. When the time comes and you must take a stand, let your voice be heard. Edmund Burke (1729-1797, British statesman and philosopher) said, "All that is necessary for the triumph of evil is that good men do nothing."

A COUNTRY can be weakened or destroyed by many things, and those attacks can come from outside forces or elements within. Theodore Roosevelt (1858-1919, 26th President of the United States of America) felt that some of the most dangerous things to a country would be from within, and he wrote warnings about those dangers that could destroy America.

> The things that will destroy America:
> 1. Prosperity at any price.
> 2. Peace at any price.
> 3. Safety first, instead of duty first.
> 4. The love of soft living.
> 5. The get rich theory of life.

━━〰━━

Scouts don't usually have to sacrifice their lives but they can be loyal to their country in other ways. Nathan Hale (1755-1776, teacher and patriot) was a man who was willing to sacrifice his life for his country.

During the Revolutionary War, after the American army had been defeated at the Battle of Long Island in New York, General Washington retreated to the northern part of Long Island. At this time, the American army was in poor spirits. Washington didn't know if the British were preparing to surround him or attack him, so he called for a volunteer to enter the British camp and find out what the British commander intended to do.

Nathan Hale, a school teacher, volunteered for the job, and on September 14, 1776 he traveled to Norwalk, Connecticut and then on to Long Island disguised as a traveling schoolmaster seeking employment. With this disguise, Nathan Hale was able to visit the British camps in Brooklyn and New York. He gained much valuable information; however, the night before he was to return, the British found out what he was doing. Early the next morning, the boat Nathan Hale was supposed to meet turned out to be a British boat. He was searched and the British troops found several notes and plans of the British camps inside his shoes. He was sentenced to be hanged the next day.

Before the noose was place around his neck, Nathan Hale was asked if he had anything to say. Standing tall, Nathan Hale spoke words that will never be forgotten, "I only regret that I have but one life to give to my country."

WE ENJOY many freedoms in America. Freedom is a precious gift that we need to recognize and protect. Daniel Webster (1782-1852, United States senator) said, "God grants liberty only to those who love it, and are always ready to guard and defend it."

JOHN HANCOCK (1737-1793, statesman and patriot) was one of the great patriots of the Revolutionary War. He was president of the convention to write the Declaration of Independence, and served as one of the delegates from Massachusetts. In fact, if you were to look at his signature at the bottom of that document, you would see that it is the largest and boldest of all the signatures. The reason he gave for such a prominent signature is so the king of England, whose eyesight was starting to fail, could easily read his name.

John Hancock was a very wealthy man, yet he was willing to sacrifice his riches for the freedom of this nation. It is said that he expended more wealth and made greater financial sacrifices than any other man. As an example, it is recorded that at one point, the American army was attacking Boston, trying to expel the British who possessed the town at the time. During a war council, the American officers proposed a plan to destroy the city. Had this plan been executed, John Hancock would have lost his entire fortune. Yet, when the plan was presented to him, John Hancock declared his readiness to surrender it all if the liberation of his country should require it.

After the freedom of this nation was established, John Hancock continued by serving on the committee to frame the constitution for the state of Massachusetts, and also served as its first governor. John Hancock showed the spirit of true patriotism and set an outstanding example of service and sacrifice for all Americans to follow.

THE LAST SENTENCE of the Declaration of Independence reads, "And for the support of this Declaration, with a firm reliance on the protection of divine Providence, we mutually pledge to each other our Lives, our Fortunes and our sacred Honor." But what kind of men were these who signed the Declaration of Independence? Out of the 56, twenty-four of them were lawyers, eleven were merchants, and nine were farmers and large plantation owners. These were men of means—wealthy, and well educated. These men knew what they were doing when they created this document, and they knew what it meant to sign it.

They valued liberty enough that they were willing to sacrifice their lives, their wealth, and their honor if necessary.

So what happened to these men? Five were captured by the British, and tortured before they died. Twelve had their homes ransacked and burned. Two lost sons while serving in the army and another two men had sons captured. Nine died from wounds or hardships of the Revolutionary War. Eight men had their properties looted. At least two of them died penniless and bankrupt.

Several lost their wealth and others lost their lives, but each one proved they were men of honor. They showed us that freedom isn't free, and the signers of the Declaration of Independence were among those that paid the price so that we could enjoy liberty today.

—— m ——

SOMETIMES WE TAKE for granted the men and women that sacrificed their lives for this country. There were many soldiers who gave up their futures so each of us could have our own futures. There stands a monument at Guadalcanal where, during World War II, a U.S. Marine regiment was totally annihilated. The inscription reads: "When you go home, tell them, and say, 'For their tomorrows, we gave our today.'"

—— m ——

COURAGE AND UNSELFISHNESS are a rare combination. During a time of crisis this combination can save lives. There was one unknown man who became a hero because of his courage and unselfishness. This is his story.

It was late winter in Washington, D.C. A severe storm delayed all flights for the last several hours, but one flight was finally heading toward the runway, and preparing to take off.

As he received clearance to take off, the pilot revved up the engines, and then released the brakes. The plane started its normal acceleration, but as the pilot pulled back on the yoke, the nose of the plane started to raise sluggishly. A little more power, a little more speed, and everything should be all right. But the plane wasn't lifting off the runway.

All of a sudden, it was too late. There wasn't enough runway left to abort the takeoff as the plane was going too fast, and the pilot knew exactly what was wrong — ice on the wings. Moments later, the plane plunged into the icy waters of the Potomac River.

As the plane crashed, the fuselage broke in half and began to fill with water. The shock of the crash combined with the shock of the cold water prevented most of the passengers from unbuckling their seat belts. However, there were a few who were able to get out of their seats. For them, the real struggle was just beginning. Could they live long enough in the icy waters until help could come?

Almost immediately, paramedics, firemen, and policemen were dispatched to the scene, and within moments, a rescue helicopter hovered over the river where the plane had gone down. There, holding on to some floating wreckage, were several survivors. The helicopter had a rescue harness attached to a cable that it could lower. However, the harness could only pick up one person at a time.

As the helicopter lowered the harness, a man grabbed it, and handed it to the person next to him. He helped the person into the harness, then the helicopter lifted that person out of the icy water, and over to the shore where paramedics waited to rush that person to the hospital.

The helicopter returned and again lowered the harness. Again, the same man grabbed it, and gave it to the person next to him. One more person was saved from an icy grave. This happened several times, and each time the same man grabbed the harness, and gave it to neighbor, saving the neighbor's life.

Finally, the helicopter returned to pick up the last man—the one who had previously grabbed the harness each time and passed it on to someone else. But as the helicopter returned and shined the spotlight on the floating debris in the river, the man was no longer there. The spotlight quickly swept up and down the river, then it swept along the banks of the river—but nothing. The man who had so unselfishly helped others was nowhere to be found. He had given the ultimate sacrifice. There were only a few bodies pulled out of that river that were not in their seat belts. That man, whoever he was, must have been one of them.

———⚬———

IT TAKES COURAGE to risk your life for something that is more important than anything else in this world. There aren't very many things like that, but every person should have family, friends, values, and ideals that they hold close to their hearts. Theodore Roosevelt (1858-1919, 26th President of the United States of America) said, "No man is worth his salt who is not ready at all times to risk his body, to risk his well-being, to risk his life in a great cause."

———— ∿ ————

SOMETIMES WE'RE afraid to try something because it is new and unfamiliar. Sometimes we're afraid to try because we don't want to fail. Whatever the reason, you'll never know if it is something you'll succeed in or something you're good at unless you take that first step and try. Theodore Roosevelt (1858-1919, 26th President of the United States of America) said, "Far better is it to dare mighty things, to win glorious triumphs, even though checkered by failure, than to take rank with those poor spirits who neither enjoy much nor suffer much, because they live in the gray twilight that knows not victory nor defeat."

———— ∿ ————

HAVE YOU EVER noticed that in most races, the difference between first and second place is just a fraction of a second? The same is true in school. In most cases the difference between an A and a B grade is just a couple of points. So how do you turn a B grade into an A grade, or a second place into first place? The difference is in the extra effort. Learn to run an extra lap when you're tired and everyone else is done for the day. Or do a few problems more than what the teacher assigned so you know you understand the subject completely. The champions are the ones that put forth that extra effort.

THE CHAMPION

The average runner sprints
Until the breath in him is gone;
But the champion has the iron will;
That makes him carry on.

For rest, the average runner begs,
When limp his muscles grow;
But the champion runs on leaden legs
His spirit makes him go.

The average man's complacent
When he does his best to score;
But the champion does his best
And then he does a little more.

AUTHOR UNKNOWN

———〜〜———

ABRAHAM LINCOLN (1809-1865, 16th President of the United States of America) was known for his perseverance. He was a successful person, but he didn't always succeed at everything he did. He had his share of failures, but he didn't give up. Instead, he worked hard and kept trying.

Abraham Lincoln started as a successful lawyer, but faced his share of challenges. For example, the first time he ran for the state legislature, he was defeated—but he didn't give up. He was defeated at his first attempt to be nominated for Congress—but he didn't give up. He was defeated when he applied to be appointed Commissioner of the Land Office—but he didn't give up. He was defeated when he ran again for the state legislature—but he didn't give up. He was defeated in his nomination for vice president—but he didn't give up. And he was defeated when he ran for the Senate—but he still didn't give up. Finally in 1860, Abraham Lincoln ran for president and won.

Remember that success doesn't always come right away. Believe in yourself, and don't give up when you're faced with failure.

THE CROWD will take the easy road, and follow the path of least resistance. Leaders need to be different. They need to dare to walk where the ground is rough, or where the path is unclear. Leaders need to forget about what the crowd may say and pursue the things that they know to be right. Edgar A. Guest (1881-1959, poet and writer) says this about those who aren't afraid to be alone.

THE FEW

The easy roads are crowded,
And the level roads are jammed;
The pleasant little rivers
With the drifting folks are crammed.
But off yonder where it's rocky,
Where you get a better view,
You will find the ranks are thinning
And the travelers are few.

Where the going's smooth and pleasant
You will always find the throng,
For the many, more's the pity,
Seem to like to drift along.
But the steeps that call for courage,
And the task that's hard to do,
In the end result in glory
For the never-wavering few.

———✠———

MANY TIMES in this life we must answer for what we've done. We must show whether our intentions and actions are true. This is called accountability, and anyone who has responsibilities is accountable and must answer for what they've done with those responsibilities.

John F. Kennedy (1917-1963, 35th President of the United States of America) said, "Of those to whom much is given, much is required. And when at some future date the high court of history sits in judgment on each one of us—recording whether in our brief span of service we fulfilled our responsibilities to the state—our success or failure . . . will be measured by the answers to four questions— were we truly men of courage . . . were we truly men of judgment . . . were we truly men of integrity . . . were we truly men of dedication?

———✠———

IT TAKES COURAGE and commitment, and to give up things like fame, money, and a successful career to do what you know in your heart is the right thing to do. Pat

Tillman (1976-2004), professional athlete and soldier) possessed that kind of courage and commitment.

Pat seemed to be an ordinary guy, but he wasn't; he was a little bit better than that. He was the type of guy that heroes are made of. Pat Tillman was born in San Jose, California. He loved to play football, and after high school, he went to Arizona State where he did very well playing college football. In 1998, he was drafted by the NFL and played for the Cardinals where in the year 2000 he broke the franchise record for the number of tackles. In 2002, he was offered a multi-million-dollar contract to continue playing for the Cardinals. However, after the tragic events of September 11, 2001, Pat Tillman strongly felt it his duty to leave the NFL and join the military.

Pat Tillman joined the U.S. Army, and became a ranger. He was ordered to serve in Afghanistan where in April 2004 he paid the ultimate price and gave his life. He died leading a team of soldiers trying to rescue fellow soldiers who had been caught in an ambush. Pat Tillman was an athlete, but even more important, he had courage and a sense of duty, and he did what he knew needed to be done.

IT TAKES COURAGE to face failure and defeat, starting over again after losing everything. Thomas Edison (1847-1931, inventor) had that kind of courage.

Thomas Edison was one of the greatest inventors in America, credited with building and developing more than a thousand different inventions. He was so successful, that he built a large laboratory complex in New Jersey. This complex had fourteen buildings, and it was there that Thomas Edison, along with his staff, did all their work. Thomas Edison was also known for his determination and hard work, and the positive attitude. Everyone thought of him as a genius, but he called his success hard work. He said, "Genius is ninety-nine percent perspiration and one percent inspiration." He was also positive and tried to build up others. If he believed in something, he would not give up in the face of failure. He was quoted as saying, "Many of life's failures are people who did not realize how close they were to success when they gave up."

In December of 1914, his laboratory caught on fire. He was 67 at the time, old enough to quit and retire, but that wasn't his way. Instead, as the fire was burning, Thomas Edison said, "Kids, go get your mother. She'll never see another fire like this one." Using his positive outlook on life, Thomas Edison set out to rebuild his lab, because he still felt like he had too much left to do. He continued working and inventing for another seventeen years before he finally passed away at the age of 84.

SOMETIMES THE BLAME for something lands on you, but it isn't your fault. Or perhaps your words are altered to make you look like a liar, but you're not. One day, you might be with a group of people who will try to make you bend, and you'll have to hold your ground. One part of courage is keeping your wits about you enough so that you don't fall into a "trap for fools."

If

If you can keep your head when all about you
Are losing theirs and blaming it on you;
If you can trust yourself when all men doubt you,
But make allowance for their doubting too;
If you can wait and not be tired by waiting,
Or, being lied about, don't deal in lies,
Or, being hated, don't give way to hating,
And yet don't look too good, nor talk too wise;

If you can dream—and not make dreams your master;
If you can think—and not make thoughts your aim;
If you can meet with triumph and disaster
And treat those two impostors just the same;
If you can bear to hear the truth you've spoken
Twisted by knaves to make a trap for fools,
Or watch the things you gave your life to broken,
And stoop and build 'em up with worn-out tools;

If you can make one heap of all your winnings
And risk it on one turn of pitch-and-toss,
And lose, and start again at your beginnings
And never breathe a word about your loss;
If you can force your heart and nerve and sinew
To serve your turn long after they are gone,
And so hold on when there is nothing in you
Except the Will which says to them: "Hold on";

If you can talk with crowds and keep your virtue,

Or walk with kings—nor lose the common touch;
If neither foes nor loving friends can hurt you;
If all men count with you, but none too much;
If you can fill the unforgiving minute
With sixty seconds' worth of distance run—
Yours is the Earth and everything that's in it,
And—which is more—you'll be a Man, my son!

RUDYARD KIPLING
(1865-1936, POET AND AUTHOR)

———~m~———

WHAT IS COURAGE and how do you recognize it? Does a brave man come by his courage automatically?

Eddie Rickenbacker (1890-1973, Pilot and businessman) was a brave man and known as the American Ace of Aces. He faced the challenges in his life with enthusiasm and determination, despite the difficulties that life placed before him. At the age of twelve, his father died. Being one of eight children, Eddie Rickenbacker quit school to help support his family. He brought in money by doing many things, including selling newspapers and eggs. Later, he worked in a glass factory, a shoe factory, and a foundry. As a teenager, he wanted to work for an automobile company, so he offered to work for free as a janitor. The managers at the head of the company were so impressed with his eagerness that they soon promoted him to a mechanic. At age 22, Eddie Rickenbacker began racing, and two years later he set the world speed record at the Daytona Raceway in 1914.

When World War I broke out, Eddie Rickenbacker tried to enlist as a pilot, but he was too old and undereducated, so he became a chauffeur for Colonel Billy Mitchell. He convinced his superiors to send him to flying school where he became a head mechanic. Eddie Rickenbacker soon had an opportunity to fly and quickly excelled as a pilot. By the end of the war, he had survived 134 aerial encounters with the enemy, and logged more combat hours flying than any other American pilot. He had also earned the Medal of Honor, eight Distinguished Service Crosses, and the French Legion of Honor. Because of his skill as a pilot, the American press nicknamed him the American Ace of Aces. When reporters asked Eddie Rickenbacker about his courage in combat, he admitted that he had been afraid, but then he said, "Courage is doing what you're afraid to do. There can be no courage unless you're scared."

SOME OF THE GREATEST things ever accomplished are things that have never been done before. Scientist, inventors, explorers, and businessmen have all made our lives better because they weren't afraid to try something new. Edgar Guest (1881-1959, poet and writer) wrote a poem where he challenges us not to follow the beaten path, but to have courage and do something that hasn't been done before.

THE THINGS THAT HAVEN'T BEEN DONE BEFORE

The things that haven't been done before,
    Those are the things to try;
Columbus dreamed of an unknown shore
    At the rim of the far-flung sky,
And his heart was bold and his faith was strong
    As he ventured in dangers new,
And he paid no heed to the jeering throng
    Or the fears of the doubting crew.

The many will follow the beaten track
    With guideposts on the way.
They live and have lived for ages back
    With a chart for every day.
Someone has told them it's safe to go
    On the road he has traveled o'er,
And all that they ever strive to know
    Are the things that were known before.

A few strike out, without map or chart,
    Where never a man has been,
From the beaten paths they draw apart
    To see what no man has seen.
There are deeds they hunger alone to do;
    Though battered and bruised and sore,
They blaze the path for the many, who
    Do nothing not done before.

The things that haven't been done before
    Are the tasks worthwhile today;
Are you one of the flock that follows; or
    Are you one that shall lead the way?
Are you one of the timid souls that quail
    At the jeers of a doubting crew,
Or dare you, whether you win or fail,
    Strike out for a goal that's new?

SOMETIMES IT'S EASY to say that a Scout is brave, but in life that can be easier to say than to do. It's especially hard to be brave when discouraged or depressed, yet that's exactly what we should do. It takes courage to keep trying when everything is going wrong and you feel like quitting. Edmund Burke (1729-1797, British statesman and philosopher) said, "Never despair, but if you do, work on in despair." Some of your sweetest rewards and greatest triumphs will come when you keep trying, even though you feel like you want to quit.

OTHERS

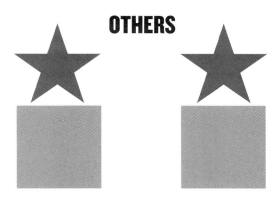

A Scout is **HELPFUL**. A Scout is concerned about other people. He does things willingly for others without pay or reward.

A Scout is **FRIENDLY**. A Scout is a friend to all. He is a brother to other Scouts, and all the people of the world. He seeks to understand others. He respects those with ideas and customs other than his own.

A Scout is **COURTEOUS**. A Scout is polite to everyone. He knows that good manners make it easier for people to get along together.

A Scout is **KIND**. A Scout understands there is strength in being gentle. He treats others as he wants to be treated. He is not cruel to living things.

A SCOUT MUST LEARN TO WORK HARD. Lessons can be learned from hard work. Those who can work hard and finish what they start are the same ones that win "life's victories."

> Stick to your task till it sticks to you
> Beginners are many, but enders are few.
> Honor, power, place and praise
> Will come in time to him who stays.
>
> Stick to your task till it sticks to you
> Bend at it, sweat at it, smile at it too;
> For out of the bend, the sweat, and the smile
> Will come life's victories, after awhile.

AUTHOR UNKNOWN

THE SCOUT slogan is to do a good turn daily. We should all do at least one good turn a day, but is that enough? John Wesley John Wesley (1703-1791, Anglican clergyman and evangelist) said:

> Do all the good you can
> By all the means you can
> In all the ways you can
> In all the places you can
> At all the times you can
> To all the people you can
> As long as ever you can.

ONE OF THE GREAT attributes of Scouting is that it teaches young men to work together to achieve a common goal. A team can always do more by working together than they can do by working individually. Teamwork can bring out the best in all who are involved. An amazing example of this can be found in the story of the Apollo 13 mission to the moon.

Almost fifty-six hours into the flight, the crew felt a sudden explosion. They were 205,000 miles from Earth, and alarms were ringing through the cabin of the spaceship. The spacecraft was losing power and oxygen. The astronauts, Jim Lovell, (1928, Eagle Scout and astronaut), Jack Swigert, and Fred Haise were in grave danger.

Up to this point there had been four missions to the moon with the last two landing on the moon. This was to be the third moon landing—but not anymore. The astronauts were still headed to the moon, but with the sudden emergency it would take a huge effort and a lot of teamwork just to bring them back to Earth.

The spacecraft that made up Apollo 13 was actually three separate modules all linked together: the service module, the command module, and the lunar module. The service module contained the fuel, oxygen, water, and electricity; but it had exploded and was now useless. Without it, Apollo 13 couldn't fire its main engine. It would helplessly swing around the moon and miss the earth by 4,000 miles.

Teams on the ground went to work. The engineers and scientists only had hours to perform the calculations that usually took weeks. They tested their results and sent the information to the crew. The engine on the lunar module was used to put the ship on a course that would bring them back to the earth.

Other problems still loomed. The spacecraft's regular air supply was gone, and while the lunar module contained enough air to get them back to Earth, they somehow had to clean the carbon dioxide out of the air supply. Again, teams went to work and a solution was found.

After four days, and a trip around the moon, the astronauts needed to direct the command module to enter the earth's atmosphere. They needed to turn on the computers, but if they did it in the wrong order they would overload the batteries and lose all power and computers. Engineers spent long days figuring how to turn on everything without overloading the batteries.

The three astronauts landed safely in the Pacific Ocean. Flight commander Jim Lovell, called the Apollo 13 mission a failure, but he added, "I like to think that it was a successful failure." It truly was a successful failure because of the teams of scientists, engineers, and astronauts that worked out solutions to extremely difficult problems so the astronauts could return home safely.

WHAT WOULD you do if you were alone on a dusty road, and there in front of you lay a bag full of money? Would you keep it, or would try to find the owner? Many years ago, a young man was driving his wagon on an empty road when he found $2,000 in cash. There was no one in sight, so he picked it up, got back in his wagon and drove on. He had traveled down the road a bit when he came across a sad and distraught gentleman. He stopped and asked the man if he needed help. The gentle man told him he'd lost his company's payroll. The young man in the wagon asked him a few more questions and then realized that the bag of money belonged to him. He returned it to the gentleman, for which the gentleman was very grateful.

SOMETIMES we feel like we can't do very much by ourselves. We feel like we are just one person, and what can one person do? Edward Everett Hale (1822-1909, author and clergyman) wrote the following poem that shows that even one person can make a difference.

ONE

I am only one
But I am one;
I cannot do everything
But I can do something,
And what I can do
That I ought to do;
And what I ought to do
By the grace of God,
I will do.

To advance in rank in Scouting, a Scout must perform service. A Scout learns to serve his fellow man, to serve his community, and to serve those in need. But how can we serve God? Benjamin Franklin (1706-1790, printer, inventor, and statesman) said, "The most acceptable service to God is doing good to man."

We serve God by serving our fellow man. And we serve our fellow man best by caring about them and helping them when they are in trouble or in need. Henry van Dyke (1852-1933, pastor and author) said:

> Who seeks for heaven alone to save his soul,
> May keep the path, but will not reach the goal;
> While he who walks in love may wander far,
> Yet God will bring him where the blessed are.

God has given this Earth to us to enjoy. It is our duty to take care of it, but it is also our privilege to enjoy its beauty. There is so much to enjoy that we would be very shallow if we only focused on a small part and paid no attention to everything else that surrounded us. Maltbie D. Babcock (1858-1901, minister and poet) said, "Life is what we are alive to. It is not length but breadth. To be alive only to appetite, pleasure, pride, money-making, and not to goodness, kindness, purity, love, history, poetry, music, flowers, stars, God, and eternal hope is to be all but dead."

A MAN'S 9-year-old son taught him a very interesting lesson. They were driving to the university for his piano competition, and as they were driving, the dad commented that someone had left 14 cents in the cup holder. He said that 14 cents wasn't very much, and that he couldn't even buy a candy bar with fourteen cents. The father and son talked about what little they could buy for that money. Then the boy made a very insightful observation: 14 cents wasn't very much, he said, but if you wanted to buy something for $6.14, and you only had $6.00, then that 14 cents makes all the difference in the world.

The same thing applies when we are given an assignment, and others are depending on us to fulfill that assignment. Even though it may be a small contribution, it may still be just enough to spell the difference between the overall success or failure of the project. After all, can you imagine a brick wall with one brick missing just because its contribution is small?

A LEADER must know right from wrong, and have the strength to do what's right. Abraham Lincoln (1809-1865, 16th President of the United States of America) said it this way, "Let us have faith that right makes might, and in that faith let us dare to do our duty as we understand it."

FOR THE FATHERS, mothers, bothers, sisters, and wives that worked on the production lines at home during World War II, there was a special incentive that outweighed everything else: the possibility that their own handiwork might somehow directly affect the life of a loved one. They relished the story of a seaman named Elgin Staples, whose ship went down in the Pacific Ocean. Staples was swept over the side of his ship; but he survived thanks to a life belt that proved, on later examination, to have been inspected, packed, and stamped back home in Akron, Ohio, by his own mother.

MANY COUNTRIES show respect for an unknown soldier. The unknown soldier represents all of the soldiers who have died defending and protecting their countries. In Great Britain at Westminster Abbey, there is a monument to an unknown soldier, and a plaque on that monument carries this inscription: "They buried him among the kings because he had done good toward God and toward his house." Live worthy to be buried among kings.

IF YOU FEEL like you have a good idea, stick with it. This story is an example of how persistence paid off and benefited the country as a result.

In the late 1950s, the United States was about to add two more territories, Alaska and Hawaii, as states to the union.

This presented a small problem to Congress. You see, Congress is responsible for the design of the flag, and how the white stars appear on the blue background. With 48 states, it was easy to show the 48 stars as six rows with eight stars in each row. But how do you add two more stars and still have a respectable pattern? A teacher in Lancaster, Ohio gave this problem to his class as a school project. A student by the name of Robert Heft had an idea. He thought that if the pattern alternated between a row of six stars followed by a row of five stars there would be a regular and symmetric pattern. Altogether there would be 5 rows of six stars and 4 rows of five stars, giving a total of 50 stars.

Robert Heft spent hours sewing stars onto a piece of cloth. He turned his project in, however, his teacher was unimpressed and Robert got a B-minus for his efforts. But that didn't stop Robert. He knew he had a good idea, so he sent his design to his congressman. Congress liked his idea, and as Alaska and Hawaii became the two newest states, the U.S. flag bore the design of Robert Heft, a schoolboy from Ohio.

IF SOMETHING's worth doing, it's worth doing well. Even if you have a job that seems insignificant, do your very best at it, then it will be a job you can be proud of. Oliver Wendel Homes (1809-1894, Chief Justice of the U.S. Supreme Court) said, "Every calling is great when greatly pursued. Whatever you do, do it with all your might."

IT USED TO BE that the first thing many people saw when they came to the United States was the Statue of Liberty. To them the statue represented freedom and an opportunity to start a new life.

These are the words written by Emma Lazarus (1849-1887, poet and writer), that are on the plaque at the base of the Statue of Liberty:

> "Keep, ancient lands, your storied pomp! cries she
> With silent lips. Give me your tired, your poor,
> Your huddled masses yearning to breathe free,
> The wretched refuse of your teeming shore.
> Send these, the homeless, the tempest-tossed to me;
> I lift my lamp beside the golden door."

These words can mean the same to us today, encouraging us to value our freedom and the great opportunities we have.

OUR SOCIETY will function well if we can learn to live peacefully together, and respect each other as individuals. On the other hand, there are traits that destroy the fabric of our society. It happens when people think only of themselves, and not of others. There are seven deadly sins of society. They are:

1) To live on policies without principles.

2) Wealth without work.

3) Pleasure without conscience.

4) Knowledge without character.

5) Commerce and industry without morality.

6) Science without humanity.

7) Worship without sacrifice.

They all boil down to the love of self, the love of money, and the love of power. When those become more important than sacrifice, service, and caring for others, then society will suffer.

IF YOU DO your duty, then you can make a difference. And though you are just one person, look at the power of one person in some of the important decisions that affected our nation.

It was by one vote in the electoral college that Thomas Jefferson, John Quincy Adams, and Rutherford B. Hays were elected president of the United States. And in the case of President Hays, the man who cast his deciding vote was a congressman from Indiana who was himself elected by only one vote. It was also by just one vote that California, Idaho, Oregon, Texas, and Washington were admitted as states.

THE CUB SCOUT motto is "Do your best." It's important to learn to do your best because this life gives its best to those who give their best. Madeline Bridges (1844-1920, poet) wrote a poem that shows how life mirrors what we do.

LIFE'S MIRROR

There are loyal hearts, there are spirits brave,
There are souls that are pure and true,
Then give to the world the best you have,
And the best will come back to you.

Give love, and love to your life will flow,
A strength in your utmost need.
Have faith, and a score of hearts will show
Their faith in your word and deed.

Give truth, and your gift will be paid in kind;
And honor will honor meet;
And a smile that is sweet will surely find
A smile that is just as sweet.

For life is the mirror of king and slave.
'Tis just what we are and do;
Then give to the world the best you have,
And the best will come back to you.

A LARGE PART of Scouting is service, and service has a noble purpose. Those who give service learn to think of others, learn to help those in need, and learn to put others above themselves. It is also through service that we feel a sense of fulfillment in our lives. David O. McKay (1873-1970, educator and religious leader) said, "He who lets selfishness and his passions rule him binds his soul in slavery, but he who, in the majesty of spiritual strength, uses his physical tendencies and yearnings, and his possessions to serve purposes higher than personal indulgences and comfort, takes the first step toward the happy and useful life."

A SCOUT IS HELPFUL. But do you really try to help others? Do you look for opportunities to give a hand? In many cases, when we help others, we also help ourselves. It was reported that while Andrew Carnegie was making his millions, he also helped 38 other men become millionaires.

On the other hand, there are people who always tear others down. They always criticize and try to bring others down to a lower level. It has been said that you don't need to put a lid over a basket of crabs because as soon as one starts to climb out of the basket, the others will pull it down and back into the basket.

So what kind of person do you want to be known as? A person who tears others down, or one who builds them up? To be a helpful person, you must be the one who builds.

COURTESY AND KINDNESS are things you can give away yet never lose, and as you learn to give them, they become easier to give. Most of us will have to work to earn a living and support our families and ourselves. You may make a living by what you get, but you make a life by what you give.

—⟐—

A SCOUT IS FRIENDLY. Everyone needs a friend although not everyone will show that they want a friend. We have a duty to be a friend even to those who have been hurt and are trying to be alone. It is through sincere concern that we can touch the lives of those who fight against us. Edwin Markham (1852-1940, poet and author) penned these words:

OUTWITTED

He drew a circle that shut me out-
Heretic, rebel, a thing to flout.
But love and I had the wit to win;
We drew a circle that took him in!

—⟐—

WE WON'T ALWAYS be paid for all the work that we do. In fact, there are many important things that we will do and receive no form of financial payment for it. Yet it is these actions that will bring us the greatest rewards in our lives. Albert Schweitzer (1875-1965), theologian, missionary, and doctor) said, "I don't know what your destiny will be, but one thing I know: The only ones among you who will be truly happy are those who will have sought and found how to serve."

A SCOUT LOVES to play around. He loves to play tricks on his leaders and on other Scouts. Sometimes that's good, but sometimes it isn't. As we associate with other people, we need to remember to be kind. Here is a story of how two young men decided to pull a nice trick instead of a mean one.

An older boy and his young companion were walking along a road that led through a field. They saw an old coat and a badly worn pair of men's shoes by the roadside, and in the distance they saw the owner working in the field.

The younger boy suggested that they hide the shoes, conceal themselves, and watch the perplexity on the owner's face when he returned.

The older boy thought that would not be so good, realizing that the owner must be a very poor man. So, after talking the matter over, they decided to try another experiment. Instead of hiding the shoes, they would put a silver dollar (which was then a commonly used coin) in each shoe and see what the owner did when he discovered the money.

Soon the man returned from the field, put on his coat, slipped one foot into a shoe and felt something hard. He took his foot out and found the silver dollar. Wonder and surprise shone upon his face. He looked at the dollar again and again, turned around but could see nobody. He then proceeded to put on the other shoe. When to his great surprise he found another dollar, his feelings overcame him. He knelt down and offered aloud a prayer of thanksgiving, in which he spoke of his wife being sick and helpless and his children without bread. He fervently thanked God for this bounty from unknown hands and evoked the blessing of heaven upon those who gave him this needed help.

The boys remained hidden until he had gone. They had been touched by his prayer and his sincere expression of gratitude. As they left to walk down the road, one said to the other, "Don't you have a good feeling?"

—⁓—

WE HAVE ALL given service, and while it is good to give service when asked, it is even better to serve without being asked. If you see a need, jump in and help out. Don't wait for someone to ask for your help, just do it. The story of a wise king and his beautiful highway illustrates how this is done.

A king in a faraway land decided that he would build a new road that would stretch from one end of his kingdom to the other. It would go over a large mountain, by a lake, through a forest, and pass by some beautiful villages along the way. As the road was being completed, he saw that it was going to be a magnificent road that travelers would always enjoy. And so he decided to have a special contest for those that traveled the road on opening day. The king would award a bag of gold to the person who could travel the road the best.

He sent a proclamation through his country and to all the surrounding countries inviting people to come and travel his road on its opening day. The proclamation also explained that whoever traveled the road the best on this day would be rewarded with a bag of gold.

"How can you travel the road the best?" the people asked themselves. "What did that mean?" For the remaining weeks before the completion of the road, the people pondered that question.

Finally the day arrived, and people came from all over the kingdom. Some came in their finest apparel. Others came with horses and chariots. Still others brought camels, elephants, and servants all traveling in caravans. Each sought, in their own way, to travel the road the best. Each sought to find favor with the king, and win the bag of gold.

As they journeyed, they saw that it was indeed a most beautiful road. It went over a mountain, by a lake, through a forest and passed by some beautiful villages. And at the end of the road, the king stood there to greet each traveler. And before the traveler could say anything, the king would ask, "What did you think of my road?"

The travelers would reply, "Oh, King, it is a most beautiful road. There is none to compare." But then they would add, "But King, the road is not quite complete, for at one point in the road, there is still a large pile of rocks right in the middle of the road."

At that point, the king would thank the traveler, and go on to the next traveler who was finishing his journey. Many of the travelers would prod the king, asking whether they had traveled the road the best. But the king would put them off, and simply say, "It's too early to tell, I cannot give an answer at this time."

The day wore on, and the scene continued to repeat itself. The king would ask each traveler what he thought of the road. Then each traveler would tell how beautiful it was, but then add that it was still unfinished because of the pile of rocks at the certain point. The king would thank the traveler, and then the traveler would ask if he had traveled the road the best, but the king would put off answering.

Toward evening, the travelers coming down the road had begun to thin out. Many of those that had traveled the road had gone home, knowing that the king had not recognized them as having traveled the road the best. However, most of the more pompous travelers were still waiting for the king to make his decision and award the prize.

At sunset, the king saw a lone traveler coming, and he was carrying a large heavy bag. As the man approached, the king asked him what he thought of the road. The man responded that it was a most beautiful road, but then he added: "At a certain point on the journey, I found a large pile of rocks right in the middle of the road. And I thought to myself that this road would be perfect if that pile of rocks were removed from the road. So I started removing them myself. And as I was completing my task, I found this bag of gold at the bottom of the pile of rocks. Oh, King, the road is yours and therefore this bag of gold is yours. I have come to return it to you."

At this point the king said, "No, my friend, it is yours." The king turned to all who were still waiting and said, "This man has traveled my road the best because he made it easier for others to travel. He has won the gold I promised as the prize."

He who travels the road the best is the one who makes the road easier for those who follow after him.

―――※※※―――

YOU WON'T ALWAYS agree with everyone you meet. People are different, and have different feelings about things. We need to respect those differences. If we must openly disagree, then we must learn how to disagree without being disagreeable. The more hot arguments you win, the fewer warm friends you will have. And if that's not enough, just remember, a person with a sharp tongue is likely to cut his own throat.

―――※※※―――

IT IS INTERESTING that the Scout law lists the points of being helpful and friendly right next to each other. In a way, being helpful and friendly are gifts that we can give to others. And these gifts are unique because they will cost little if anything at all; yet they can be some of the most valuable things you've ever given. An unknown poet said it this way:

> The greatest gifts you'll ever give
> Though with them never part,
> Are simply these:
> A helping hand,
> A friendly smile,
> And a selfless, loving heart.

AT TIMES WE should take a moment and think of the many blessings we have. It is a good quality to be grateful, and it is something that we should express to those around us. We should let our families, leaders, and friends know that we appreciate the work and the sacrifices that they do for us. The story of Abram and Zimri tells of two brothers who were grateful for each other.

Two brothers, Abram and Zimri, lived side by side in separate homes, yet shared a piece of land, and worked the fields together year after year. Abram had a wife and seven children, while Zimri had never married and lived alone in his humble home. Yet each year as they brought in their harvest, the two brothers would divide the hay into two equal halves, and each would take their half as their reward for their labors that year.

Then one year, Abram was lying in his bed one night thinking of all the things for which he was grateful, and how he had been so blessed. He had a wife and seven wonderful children, while his poor brother had none, yet they equally divided the harvest in half each year. Without a second thought, Abram secretly left his house, and went down to the fields. He took a heaping third off of his haystack and placed it on his brother's. Then he snuck quietly back to his home and slept peacefully the rest of the night.

As chance would have it, that very night Zimri was lying in his bed thinking of all of his wonderful blessings.

He had his health and strength, and he was always able

to help others in the community while his poor brother had to work so hard to support his wife and seven children, yet they equally divided the harvest each year. Then without a moment's hesitation, Zimri climbed out of bed, and went down to the fields where he took a heaping third off of his haystack and placed it on his brother's. He then quietly went back to bed and slept peacefully until morning.

Imagine the surprise the next morning as the two brothers walked side by side down to the fields only to find that both haystacks were exactly the same size. Neither said a word as they worked side by side that day. Then late that next night, Abram snuck quietly out of his house, and went down to the fields. He quietly took a heaping third off of his haystack and placed it on his brother's. But instead of returning to his home, he hid himself behind his haystack. It wasn't very much longer before he saw his brother coming down the road to the field. And there in the moonlight, Abram saw Zimri take a heaping third off of his own haystack and place it on Abram's. At that moment Abram stepped out from behind his haystack and gave his brother a warm embrace.

TO BE SUCCESSFUL, we need to learn how to set priorities. This means that we do the most important things first, and then if there is time we can do the things of lesser importance next. As we put first things first, remember that people are first and things are second. By putting first things first it also often means that you put yourself last.

A SCOUT IS COURTEOUS, and to truly be courteous you must be thoughtful and considerate of others. Sometimes this also means that we look out for those who don't have the ability to look our for themselves. In other words, we don't take advantage of others just because we are bigger or smarter or stronger than they are. Abraham Lincoln (1809-1865, 16th President of the United States of America) knew that it was morally wrong to take advantage of someone even if you could legally do it.

Before he became president of the United States, Abraham Lincoln practiced law, and was a very successful lawyer. On one occasion, after listening carefully to the statement of his case by a client, Abraham Lincoln said, "Yes, there is no reasonable doubt that I can win your case for you. I could distress that widowed mother and her six fatherless children, and thereby get for you that six hundred dollars, although it appears to me that it rightfully belongs to her as much as it belongs to you. However, you must remember that some things that are legally right are not morally right, and therefore I shall not take your case. Instead, I will give you some advice for which I will charge you nothing. You seem to be a sprightly, energetic man. I would advise you to try your hand at making six hundred dollars some other way."

I**T IS SAD** indeed, but many times quarrels and fights break out between family and friends because of small misunderstandings. One person believes they are right and therefore the other person must be wrong. Yet, if only they would look through another's eyes, they would see that others could be right also. How could that be? Consider the following story.

Two knights happened to meet in front of an inn in a small township one day. Not finding anything better to discuss, they spoke of the sign that hung overhead. One said that the sign was gold while the other said that it was silver. Soon an argument broke out, and as the debate became even more heated, the good knights challenged each other to a duel.

The noble warriors mounted their steeds, fixed their swords, and charged at each other. Luck was with them, for even though they both knocked each other off their horses, they both fell to the ground unhurt. Upon arising, each man found that he was looking at the opposite side of the sign for the first time. It was only then that they realized that one side of the innkeeper's sign was gold, and the other side was silver.

H**AVE YOU EVER** noticed how some people demand their rights, even if it offends another person's feelings? They say, "I have the right to say what I want," or "I have the right to do as I please." While this may be true, it's not always kind. And a true gentleman will consider the feelings of others before spouting off with such a demand. A gentleman is one who thinks more of other people's feelings than of his own rights, and more of other people's rights than his own feelings.

—m—

A SCOUT IS KIND in word and in deed, and for good reason. Aside from the fact that it is good to get along with others, this short poem explains some personal reasons why we should show kindness to others.

> Be careful of the words you say,
> And keep them soft and sweet.
> For you never know from day to day,
> Which ones you'll have to eat.

—m—

MOST PEOPLE LIKE to be independent. They like to know that they can stand on their own and work things out by themselves. However there are times when problems come. These problems take their turn and come in time to all people at sometime in their lives. As Adam Lindsay Gordon (1833-1870, author and poet) says, the best thing we can do is to show kindness to others in their time of need, and to have courage when it is our turn to face hardship and trials.

QUESTION NOT

Question not, but live and labor,
Till your goal be won,
Helping every feeble neighbor,
Seeking help from none;
Life is mostly froth and bubble,
Two things stand like stone—
Kindness in another's trouble,
Courage in our own.

———✦———

WE SERVE GOD by serving our fellowman; we sacrifice to God by making sacrifices for our fellowman; and we show our love to God by loving our fellowman. Abou Ben Adhem is the story of a man who loved his fellowman, and was blessed by God because of it.

ABOU BEN ADHEM

Abou Ben Adhem (may his tribe increase!)
Awoke one night from a deep dream of peace,
And saw, within the moonlight in his room,
Making it rich, and like a lily in bloom,
An angel writing in a book of gold:
Exceeding peace had made Ben Adhem bold,
And to the Presence in the room he said,
"What writest thou?"—The vision raised its head,
And with a look made of all sweet accord,
Answered, "The names of those who love the Lord."
"And is mine one?" said Abou. "Nay, not so,"
Replied the Angel. Abou spoke more low,

But cheerily still; and said, "I pray thee, then,
Write me as one that loves his fellow-men."
The angel wrote, and vanished. The next night
It came again with a great wakening light,
And showed the names whom the love of
    God had blessed,
And lo! Ben Adhem's name led all the rest!

JAMES HENRY LEIGH HUNT
(1784-1859, AUTHOR AND POET)

A SCOUT IS FRIENDLY. And while it is easy to be friendly with our friends, we also need to be friendly with those who don't know us, and who aren't our friends. This also means that we need to be friendly to our enemies. Although a difficult thing to do, there is a story of Abraham Lincoln (1809-1865, 16th President of the United States of America) and his unique way of dealing with his enemies.

An associate once took him to task for his kind attitude toward his enemies. His friend advised, "Why do you try to make friends of them? You should try to destroy them." To this, Lincoln gently replied, "Am I not destroying my enemies when I make them my friends?"

To BE A LEADER is to give service. A good leader has vision, and knows the way, and he serves by helping those he leads. He gives his followers direction and guidance, and then through his leadership, helps his followers accomplish their goals. True leadership can't be selfish or self-serving; instead, it is a giving of one's self and a willingness to sacrifice. Through service, a leader shines like a light so that others may follow.

The story is told of a youngster walking through a thick London fog one evening, carrying a lighted lantern. "Guide me back to my hotel," called a man from out of the fog, "and I'll give you a shilling."

"Yes, sir," said the boy, and holding his lantern high, he started walking through the fog. Upon arriving at the hotel, not one man stepped forward with a shilling, but four men. The other three had seen the light and followed it without question.

DID YOU KNOW that the more refined a piece of steel is, the more value it has? For example, scrap steel is worth very little. It is sold by the pound, and almost always sold in large quantities because it is hardly worth it to buy just a small amount. Now, if you take that scrap steel, and make it into something useful like a box of nails, you've increased the value of that steel by more than four times. Now suppose that instead of nails, you work with that steel a little more, and make it into a set of tools. The steel that you started with is now worth even more. In fact, its value now can be up to ten times the value of the nails and over forty times that of the scrap metal. Service is that refining process for your character, and education is that refining process for your mind. You will find that the more value you build within yourself, the more value you will be able to give to others.

SERVICE AND KINDNESS are often related. Through service we show kindness, and because of kindness we give service. Doing these acts of unselfishness help those who come after us. This poem by Will Allen Dromgoole (1860-1934, writer and poet) illustrates how service helps those who follow.

THE BRIDGE BUILDER

An old man going a lone highway,
Came at the evening, cold and gray,
To a chasm vast and wide and steep
With waters rolling cold and deep.
The old man crossed in the twilight dim;
The sullen stream had no fears for him;
But he turned when safe on the other side
And built a bridge to span the tide.
"Old man," said a fellow pilgrim near,
"You are wasting your strength
    with building here
Your journey will end with the ending day
You never again will pass this way;
You've crossed the chasm deep and wide,
Why build you this bridge at eventide?"

The builder lifted his old gray head,
"Good friend, in the path I have come," he said,
"There followeth after me today
A youth, whose feet must pass this way;

The chasm that was as naught to me,
To that fair-haired youth may a pitfall be;
He too must cross in the twilight dim—
Good friend, I am building this bridge for him."

NOTHING IS AS CONSTANT as change. Everything around us changes. Opportunities come and go. And best friends that we have today, while they will always be our friends, by tomorrow they may be gone to distant lands. For this reason alone, we should take every opportunity to be kind and helpful to those around us. Ralph Waldo Emerson (1803-1882, philosopher, writer, and poet) said, "You can not do a kindness too soon, for you will never know when it will be too late."

DISCIPLINE is a part of leadership, and a good leader keeps that in mind. It isn't always pleasant, but it is necessary, and in the long run, and if done in a spirit of love and concern, all are better because of it.

Sometimes we need to be reminded that there are two reasons why a leader must discipline those he leads:

The first is to make right the thing that
   was wrong.
The second is to make the person right
   that was wrong.

In other words, the mistake must be corrected, and so must the person. If property was stolen or damaged, then it should be replaced or fixed. This becomes an opportunity to teach the offender the value of property, and that he is responsible for the damage that he caused. And by taking advantage of the teaching moment, you help make the person right who was wrong.

THERE WILL ALWAYS BE someone who will come along and hurt your feelings or offend you in some way. Sometimes they will ask for your forgiveness, but sometimes they won't. Either way, you need to forgive them. If you don't, you may begin to carry resentment within your heart. This resentment can build into a bitterness that will hurt you worse than anything anyone else could have done to you. Bitterness injures the one who carries it, not the one against whom it is directed.

WHEN YOU ASK for something from your parents or a leader, sometimes you will get a no for an answer. Learn to be able to take a no as an answer and accept it and live with it.

There are people who would have you believe that you don't need to take no for an answer in anything. This is not true. Those same people would show you successful people who don't stop at anything. They get what they want no matter what the cost. And many times they have had to trade their self-respect, their virtue, and their personal integrity to get everything they want.

You don't need everything you want, and a no every once in a while will not hurt you. Having said that, you should also know that there are times when you don't have to take no as your answer. There will be many times where through your desire, persistence, negotiation, or hard work you can change a no to a yes, and if you can do it without sacrificing your integrity, your morals or your self-respect, then you are a better person for having changed that no to a yes. But be careful, and be wise. Most of the time it is good to be ambitious, but you should always be humble and grateful and trust in God, and trust that all things will work out for your good, even the no's.

IN TODAY'S WORLD, we see on the news the attacks of suicide bombers—people that blow themselves up, and throw their lives away for their cause. While it is true there are things in this life that are worth dying for, it doesn't mean that we should throw our lives away, or die needlessly. There is no cause worth dying for that is not better served by living for it. The people that kill themselves for their cause would actually do better by living for their cause and finding some productive way to promote what they believe to be right.

A Scout learns to respect his parents, his leaders, and authority. Giving proper respect means that sometimes we bite our tongue and not shout out the first thing that comes to our minds. In this way, we show respect by being courteous and kind. However, that respect must be balanced with honesty. We must learn how to disagree without being disagreeable. This story about the trip to Albuquerque illustrates why this is important.

A family was coming home from a long vacation. They had a lot of fun and saw some interesting sights. They were tired and needed to get home, yet on the way, the dad thought, "We ought to stop in Albuquerque. It is a couple of hundred miles out of our way, but I know how much it means to my wife." So he said out loud, "Who would like to go to Albuquerque?"

The mom had been thinking about going home and getting everything unpacked, when her husband asked, "Who would like to go to Albuquerque?" She hated going to Albuquerque, but she knew how much it meant to her husband, so she said out loud, "That would be wonderful. Let's go."

The kids were tired from all the traveling and playing that they had done, when their dad asked, "Who would like to go to Albuquerque?" That was the last thing they wanted to do, but the kids knew how much their parents enjoyed going to Albuquerque. They were raised to be polite, and so they waited for their mom to answer before they said anything. When their mom said, "That would be